PREPARING THE ARMY OF GOD

A Basic Training Manual For Spiritual Warfare

By

PATRICK JOSEPH HESSION

ISBN: 978-0-6152-0264-8

Cover photo by the author

Books by the author

WORDSEEDS FROM THE WILDERNESS: Calling God's People To Reconciliation, Healing, and Restoration

RECONCILIATION, HEALING, AND RESTORATION OF THE CHURCH

GOD IS YOUR FAMILY: A Key To Your True Identity And Self-Worth

INTIMATE PRAYER

PREPARING THE ARMY OF GOD: A Basic Training Manual For Spiritual Warfare

CHRISTIAN HOMEBUILDING FOR MEN

CHRISTIAN HOMEBUILDING FOR WOMEN

MEN - PLANNING FOR MARRIAGE

WOMEN - PLANNING FOR MARRIAGE

Books can be ordered by going to lulu.com and entering Hession in the Search box. The author can be contacted at familytofamilies@hotmail.com

.

TABLE OF CONTENTS

Because I love you, I want to show you what I am doing in the world today. I want to prepare you for what is to come. Days of darkness are coming on the world, days of tribulation. Buildings that are now standing will not be standing. Supports that are there for my people now will not be there. I want you to be prepared, my people, to know only me and to cleave to me and to have me in a way deeper than ever before. I will lead you into the desert. I will strip you of everything that you are depending on now so that you depend just on me. A time of darkness is coming on the world, but a time of glory is coming for my Church, a time of glory is coming for my people. I will pour out on you all the gifts of my Spirit. I will prepare you for spiritual combat. I will prepare you for a time of evangelism that the world has never seen. And, when you have nothing but me, you will have everything: land, fields, homes, and brothers and sisters and love and joy and peace more than ever before. Be ready, my people. I want to prepare you.

I speak to you of the dawn of a "new age" for my Church. I speak to you of a day that has not been seen before. Prepare yourselves for the action that I begin now because things that you see around you will change. The combat that you must enter now is different, it is new.

You need wisdom from me that you do not yet have. You need the power of my Holy Spirit in a way that you have not possessed it. You need understanding of my will and of the ways that I work that you do not yet have. Open your eyes, open your hearts to prepare yourselves for me and for the day that I have now begun.

My Church will be different, my people will be different. Difficulties and trials will come upon you. The comfort that you know now will be far from you, but the comfort that you will have is the comfort of my Holy Spirit. They will send for you to take your life, but I will support you. Come to me. Band yourselves together around me. Prepare, for I proclaim a new day, a day of victory and of triumph for your God. Behold, it is begun.

I will renew my Church. I will renew my people. I will make my people one. I am calling you to turn away from the pleasures of the world. I am calling you to turn away from the desires of the world. I am calling you

7

to turn away from seeking the approval of the world in your lives. I want to transform your lives.

I have a word for my Church. I am sounding my call. I am forming a mighty army. My power is upon them. They will follow my chosen shepherd(s). Be the shepherds I have called you to be. I am renewing my people. I will renew my Church. I will free the world. Know that I am with you, and, though you may pass through tribulations and trial, I will be with you, even to the end. I am preparing a place for you in glory. Look to me, and I will deliver you from the power of the evil one. Behold, I am with you now, all days, even till the end of time.

--Prophecy given through Dr. Ralph Martin at a Charismatic Conference in Rome, 1975

INTRODUCTION

When God called the Israelites out of Egypt and led them into the desert, they were nothing more than a multitude of slaves, untrained in warfare. Throughout their journey in the wilderness, they became a mighty army, as they grew in their covenant relationship with the God who revealed himself to them as "I AM." When they went into battle, God went with them and before them, and they were victorious over all their enemies.

You have been redeemed from the slavery of sin and brought into a new relationship with this same God. Because of this, you are now in battle for the rest of your life. Satan is out to destroy not only the Church of Jesus Christ but also you. The Church is at war, but Jesus has promised that the gates of Hell will not prevail against it. Yet, the Church must be trained and equipped for battle, and you also, as a member of the Church. That is the purpose of this book. Too often the Church does not look like an army, nor do its members look like soldiers. God is calling us to arms! It is time to respond and rise up once again to go forth into battle, individually and corporately, with our leader and lord, Jesus Christ!

Unless otherwise noted, the translation used is the New Revised Standard Version (NRSV), copyright 1989, Division of Christian Education of the National Council of Churches of Christ in the United States of America. Other translations include the New American Bible (NAB), copyright 1986, 1991 by the Confraternity of Christian Doctrine, the Revised English Bible (REB), copyright 1989 by the Oxford University Press and Cambridge University Press, the New Jerusalem Bible, copyright 1985 by

Longman & Todd Ltd. and Doubleday, and the Contemporary English Version (CEV), copyright 1995, Thomas Nelson, Inc. The aim is to provide as clear and accurate a presentation as possible.

A CALL TO SPIRITUAL WARFARE

The Lord is calling his people again to war -- Spiritual Warfare: *"Say to the nations: 'Get ready for war! Be eager to fight. Line up for battle and prepare to attack. Make swords out of plows and spears out of garden tools. Strengthen every weakling. Hurry, all you nations! Come quickly!"* (1)

The Lord himself has commanded his very best warriors and his proud heroes to show how angry he is. Listen to the noisy crowds on the mountains! Kingdoms and nations are joining forces. The Lord All-Powerful is bringing together an army for battle. From a distant land, the Lord is coming, fierce and furious. He brings his weapons to destroy the earth. (2)

(Satan) will use deceit to win followers from those who are unfaithful to God, but those who remain faithful will do everything possible to oppose him. Wise leaders will instruct many of the people. But, for a while, some of these leaders will be either killed with swords or burned alive, or else robbed of their possessions and thrown into prison. They will receive only a little help in their time of trouble, and many of their followers will be treacherous. Some of those who are wise will suffer so that God will make them pure and acceptable until the end, which will still come at the time he has decided. (3)

People who have their names written in The Book *will be protected. Everyone who has been wise will shine as bright as the sky above, and everyone who has led others to please God will shine like the stars.* (4) *Many people will have their hearts and lives made pure and clean, but those who are evil will keep on being evil and will never understand. Only the wise will understand.* (5)

Most people today, especially Christians who should know better, are not aware that there is a spiritual war going on. The Church does not look like an army in any sense of the word. Thus, Satan is having a heyday, and victims are everywhere. God is calling forth an army to fight with and for him. Are you willing to enter basic training?

(1) Joel 3:9-11

10

(2) Isaiah 13:3-5
(3) Daniel 11:32-35
(4) Daniel 12:1b, 3
(5) Daniel 12:10

THE NATURE OF THE WAR

You are involved in a war: a war not of your own choosing, a war that has been going on long before you came onto the scene, but a war that has a profound and personal effect on you. In fact, what you do about it will determine where and how you will spend eternity, for you must choose whose side you are on.

Yes, you must choose sides and, on the basis of that choice, become a winner or a loser. However, you cannot avoid the war. You are involved in it right now, whether you know it or not. So, you need to know what the war is all about and must decide whose side you are on.

What is this war in which you are involved? Well, it began when Lucifer, the bright morning star, the highest of the archangels whom God had made, decided that he was not satisfied with his position under God.

In his pride, Lucifer declared his independence: *"**I will** ascend to Heaven. **I will** raise my throne above the stars of God. **I will** sit on the mount of assembly in the far north. **I will** make myself like the Most High."* (1)

War broke out in Heaven. Michael and his angels fought against the dragon. The dragon and his angels fought back but were defeated, and there was no longer any place for them in Heaven. The great dragon was thrown down. That ancient serpent, called the Devil and Satan, the deceiver of the whole world, was thrown down to the earth, and his angels were thrown down with him. (2)

The direct challenge to God by Lucifer was over. He lost his position in Heaven next to God and was hurled down to earth. Lucifer, the "light-bearer" became Satan, the "adversary."

In his victory statement, God spoke to Lucifer: *"You were the signet of perfection, full of wisdom and perfect in beauty. You were in Eden, the garden of God. Every precious stone was your covering. On the day that you were created, they were prepared. You were on the holy mountain of God. You walked among the stones of fire. You were blameless in your ways from the day that you were created until iniquity was found in you. In the abundance of your trade, you were filled with violence and sinned. So, I cast you as a profane thing from the mountain of God, and the guardian cherub drove you out from among the stones of fire.*

"Your heart was proud because of your beauty. You corrupted your wisdom for the sake of your splendor. I cast you to the ground. I exposed you before kings to feast their eyes on you.

"By the multitude of your iniquities, in the unrighteousness of your trade, you profaned your sanctuaries. So, I brought out fire from within you. It consumed you, and I turned you to ashes on the earth in the sight of all who saw you.

"All who know you among the peoples are appalled at you. You have come to a dreadful end and will be no more forever.

"Will you still say, 'I am a god?'" (3)

"Yet, down to the nether world you go to the recesses of the pit! When they see you, they will stare, pondering over you: 'Is this the one who made the earth tremble and kingdoms quake? Who made the world a desert, razed its cities, and give his captives no release?'" (4)

Yes, the direct challenge was ended. Judgment was pronounced. But, the war is not yet over. Unable to go against God himself, Satan went to war against God's highest creature, human beings; human beings, whom God took special care and counsel to make in his own image and likeness; human beings, who were given lordship and dominion over all of God's creation; human beings, who were to be rulers and kings under God and, more than that, children of God, bearing the family resemblance of their Father.

Seeing that resemblance to God, God's enemy, Satan went to war. He offered to human beings the same status he had claimed for himself. Notice his strategy as recorded in Chapter 3 of the Book of Genesis:

1. He raised the question: did you hear God correctly? *"Did God tell you not to eat fruit from any tree in the garden?"* (5)

2. Eve answered correctly. *"God said we could eat fruit from any tree in the garden except the one in the middle. He told us not to eat fruit from that tree or even to touch it. If we do, we will die."* (6) Yes, Adam and Eve had heard God correctly. They knew what his command to them was and the consequence of disobeying it, so they were not in doubt or ignorance.

3. Satan, then, reinterpreted God's command and made God a liar: *"You will not die for God knows that, when you eat of it, your eyes will be opened, and **you will be like God**, knowing good and evil."* (7)

Now God knew, because he was already at war, that disobedience would mean death for human beings as it had for Satan. That is why the order of Chapter 2, verse 16 - *"You may freely eat of every tree of the garden, but of the tree of the knowledge of good and evil you will not eat because, in the day that you eat of it, you will die."* - was both a command and a warning. God knew that human beings would only find their perfect fulfillment in "freedom of obedience," not in "freedom of choice."

13

When man and woman opted for "freedom of choice" over "freedom of obedience," they, like Satan, became the next casualty. *God formed human beings to be imperishable; in the image of his own nature he made them. But, by the envy of the devil, death entered the world, and they who are in its possession experience it.* (8) And so, the judgment pronounced first upon Lucifer is now pronounced upon human beings.

From that point on, the prince of the fallen angels became also the prince of this world. From that point on, every man and woman has been born behind enemy lines. Instead of being begotten in the image of God, we are now begotten in the image of Satan. That is because, in choosing to listen to and to obey Satan, our first parents yielded their, and our, authority and dominion over all creation to him.

Thus, when you were born, you were born in enemy territory. At your best, you could only be a prisoner of war in that territory. But, it is worse than that. Reflecting the image of your master, Satan, you were a willing servant of his army and a dedicated enemy of God's army, as you chose to do your own will, your own "thing." You were separated from the God whom you were created to serve and whose nature and dominion you were given to share. Spiritually, you were dead, and there was no way in your own power that you could do anything about it.

However, the "GOOD NEWS" is that into your situation came Jesus Christ, God's own Son. He came to replace the "I will not" of man and of Satan with the "I will" of perfect obedience.

When you read the Gospels, the Good News, carefully, you will notice that Jesus never exercised "freedom of choice." His life was a perfect, unselfish, "I will" to his Father: *My food is to do the will of him who sent me and to complete his work.* (9) *I have not come down from Heaven to do my own will but the will of him who sent me.* (10) *I can do nothing on my own. As I hear, I judge, and my judgment is just because I seek to do not my own will but the will of him who sent me.* (11)

Even when he came to the end of his work and was agonizing in the garden of Gethsemane in the face of his impending crucifixion and death, Jesus chose submission and obedience: *"My Father, if it is possible, let this cup pass from me; yet, **not what I want but what you want.**"* (12) *"My Father, if this cannot pass unless I drink it, **your will** be done."* (13)

Jesus exercised the "freedom of obedience" that God wanted from human beings. His life was also a perfect "I will" to his fellow human beings: He said to Simon, who is called Peter, and Andrew, his brother, *"Follow me, and **I will make you fish for people.**"* (14) *"**I will come and cure him,**"* he said to the Roman centurion. (15) *"You are Peter, and on this rock **I will build my Church**. . .**I will give** you the keys of the kingdom of Heaven."* (16)

Jesus, the obedient Son, is Lord of Heaven and earth. Jesus is

14

declared Lord because of his obedience.

Though he was in the form of God, he did not regard equality with God as something to be exploited but emptied himself, taking the form of a slave, being born in human likeness. And, being found in human form, he humbled himself and became obedient to the point of death - even death on a Cross. Therefore, God also highly exalted him and gave him the Name that is above every name so that, at the Name of Jesus, every knee should bend, in Heaven (angels and saints) *and on earth* (humans) *and under the earth* (Satan's army)*, and every tongue should confess that Jesus Christ is Lord, to the glory of the Father.* (17)

Jesus Christ is Lord only because he freely submitted himself to the will of his Father. You must do the same if you have not yet submitted yourself to the will of the Father. You must do the same daily if you have. You who are spiritually dead must first allow yourself to be re-born of God. Jesus says, *"Very truly I tell you, no one can see the kingdom of God without being born from above or born anew. No one can enter the kingdom of God* (get out from behind enemy lines) *without being born of water and Spirit. What is born of flesh is flesh, and what is born of the Spirit is spirit."* (18)

God so loved the world that he gave his only Son so that everyone who believes in him may not perish but have eternal life. Indeed, God did not send his Son into the world to condemn the world but to save it. Those who believe in him are not condemned, but those who have not believed are condemned already because they have not believed in the name of the only Son of God. (19) Jesus said again, *"I am the gate for the sheep. Whoever enters by me will be saved and will come in and go out and find pasture. The thief* (Satan) *comes only to steal and kill and destroy. I came that they may have life and have it abundantly."* (20)

This is as clear as the command about the tree of the knowledge of good and evil back in the garden. Your choice, as theirs, is to obey or to let Satan reinterpret the words of Jesus to you. Your judgment is based on the choice you make. The proof of your faith is always your obedience, your "will."

And so, to you and to me Jesus says, *"Come to me, all you that are weary and are carrying heavy burdens, and I will give you rest. Take my yoke upon you and learn from me because I am gentle and humble in heart, and you will find rest for your souls. My yoke is easy and my burden is light."* (21)

To you and to me Jesus says, *"Everyone who acknowledges me before others, I will acknowledge before my Father in Heaven, but whoever denies me before others, I also will deny before my Father in Heaven."* (22)

To you and to me Jesus says, "Lay down your arms and surrender. Come, join my army. Go free. Give up your 'freedom of choice' that brings rebellion and death and exercise the 'freedom of obedience' that I gave you in the beginning." In this, you will find your salvation because the purpose of salvation is to bring you into obedient, willing submission to the Lordship of Jesus Christ now and for all eternity.

"In him we have redemption through his blood, the forgiveness of our transgressions according to the riches of his grace that he lavished on us. With all wisdom and insight, (the Father) has made know to us the mystery of his will according to his good pleasure that he set forth in Christ as a plan for the fullness of time, to gather up all things in him, things in Heaven and things on earth. In Christ, we have also obtained an inheritance, having been destined according to the purpose of him who accomplishes all things according to his counsel and will so that we might live for the praise of his glory." (23)

"He (Jesus) is the image of the invisible God, the firstborn of all creation. In him, all things in Heaven and on earth were created, things visible and invisible, whether thrones or dominions or rulers or powers -- all things have been created through him and for him. He himself is before all things, and in him all things hold together. He is the Head of the Body, the Church. He is the beginning, the firstborn from the dead so that he might come to have first place in everything. In him, all the fullness of God was pleased to dwell, and through him, God was pleased to reconcile to himself all things, whether on earth or in Heaven, by making peace through the blood of his Cross." (24)

You and I were once alienated from him. You still are if you have not surrendered and committed yourself to him as Savior *and* Lord. You and I, *"who were once estranged and hostile in mind, doing evil deeds, he has now reconciled in his fleshly body through death so as to present us holy and blameless and irreproachable before him -- provided that we continue securely established and steadfast in the faith without shifting from the hope promised by the gospel that we heard, which has been proclaimed to every creature under Heaven."* (25)

Yes, *"when we were dead in transgressions and the un-circumcision of our flesh* (when we were imprisoned behind enemy lines), *God made us alive together with him, when he forgave us all our transgressions, erasing the record that stood against us with its legal demands. He set this aside, nailing it to the cross. He disarmed the rulers and authorities* (Satan's army) *and made a public example of them, triumphing over them in it."* (26)

I pray that *"the God of our Lord Jesus Christ, the Father of glory, may give you a spirit of wisdom and revelation as you come to know him so that, with the eyes of your heart enlightened, you may know what is the hope to which he has called you, what are the riches of his glorious inheritance among the saints, and what is the immeasurable greatness of his power for us who believe, according to the working of his great power. God put this power to work in Christ when he raised him from the dead and seated him at his right hand in the heavenly places, far above all rule and authority and power and dominion and above every name that is named, not only in this age but also in the age to come."* (27)

The fundamental question of all life is: Who is going to be God? Salvation is the victory walk of the army of God. The basic question of salvation is not "when *were* you saved" but rather "are you letting Jesus the *Savior*, through the holy Spirit whom he has sent, bring you under the rule of Jesus the *Lord*?" Are you really committed to the Army of Jesus Christ? Or are you being a double agent, trying to serve in both armies?

Jesus says, *"Whoever does the will of my Father in heaven is my brother and sister and mother."* (28) *"If any want to become my followers, let them deny themselves and take up their cross and follow me. Those who want to save their life* (that is, do their own thing) *will lose it, and those who lose their life for my sake* (by submitting it to the Lordship of Jesus) *will find it.* (29)

Salvation is not complete until Jesus is Lord of every area of your life that is under your conscious control. Jesus wants to be Lord of your *whole* life: your spouse, your children, your job, your hopes, and your dreams. The yielding of your will that brings salvation in the first place is the same ongoing yielding that brings you under the Lordship of Jesus. To the extent that you refuse to yield, to that extent you are still in rebellion against the will of God in that area of your life.

That is why Jesus says, *"Not everyone who says to me, 'Lord, Lord' will enter the kingdom of Heaven but only the one who does the will of my Father in Heaven. On that day* (of judgment)*, many will say to me, 'Lord, Lord, did we not prophesy in your Name, and cast out demons in your Name and do many deeds of power in your Name?' Then I will declare to them, 'I never knew you; go away from me, you evildoers.' "* (30)

That is why he also says, *"We know that God does not listen to sinners* (that is, to those in rebellion) *but does listen to one who worships him and obeys his will."* (31)

If you cannot submit to the Lordship of Jesus, it will be impossible for you to submit to any authority he places over you or to your brother or sister in any part of the Body of Christ, the Church. The whole goal and thrust of God's activity is that every knee should bow in obedient and willful submission to him and every tongue should confess and proclaim that Jesus Christ is Lord.

Yes, the war is real! The war is daily! However you have to choose which side you are on. Victory is assured because Jesus has already overcome his enemy once and for all. But, just as the Israelites received only that part of the Promised Land for which they fought, you also still have your battles to win. Remember, though, that you don't fight alone if you choose Jesus as your Lord. He is the "Captain of the Hosts" and fights for and with you in every battle.

So, I say to you: *"Now, therefore, revere the Lord and serve him in sincerity and in faithfulness. Put away the gods that your ancestors served...and serve the Lord. If you are unwilling to serve the Lord, choose this day whom you will serve. As for me and my household, we will serve the Lord."* (32)

(1)   Isaiah 14:13 & 14
(2)   Revelation 12:6-9
(3)   Ezekiel 28: 12b-19, 9a
(4)   Isaiah 14:15, 17
(5)   Genesis 3:1
(6)   Genesis 3:2-3
(7)   Genesis 3:4
(8)   Wisdom 2:23-24
(9)   John 4:34
(10) John 6:38
(11) John 5:30
(12) Matthew 26:39
(13) Matthew 26:42
(14) Matthew 4:19
(15) Matthew 8:7
(16) Matthew 16:18-19
(17) Philippians 2:6-11
(18) John 3:3, 5-6
(19) John 3:16-18
(20) John 10:7-10
(21) Matthew 11:28-30
(22) Matthew 10:32-33
(23) Ephesians 1:7-12
(24) Colossians 1:15-20
(25) Colossians 1:21-23
(26) Colossians 2:13-15
(27) Ephesians 1:18-21
(28) Matthew 12:50
(29) Matthew 16:24-25
(30) Matthew 7:21-23
(31) John 9:31
(32) Joshua 24:14-15

SURVEYING THE BATTLEFIELD

According to the Children's Defense Fund*, every day in the USA, 2,556 children are born out of wedlock; 2,989 children see their parents divorce; 1,849 children are abused or neglected; 3,388 children run away from home; 1,629 children are in adult jails; 1,512 teenagers drop out of school; 10 children are killed, 30 are wounded by guns; 6 teenagers commit suicide, 437 children are arrested for drinking or drunken driving; 211 children are arrested for drug abuse; 7,742 teenagers become sexually active; 623 teenagers get syphilis or gonorrhea; 2,795 teens (women under 20) get pregnant; 1,106 teens have abortions; 372 teens miscarry; 689 babies are born to women who have had inadequate prenatal care; 791 babies are born at low birth weight (less than 5 lbs., 8 oz.); 67 babies die before their first birthday; 27 children die from poverty.

An Associated Press article, dated May 2, 1994, read as follows: The number of murders rose 3% last year, but violent crimes overall edged lower, the FBI reported Sunday, reflecting what one criminologist called the "lull before the storm." "This may be the last good report that we see in a long time," said Jack Levin, professor of Sociology and Criminology at Northeastern University in Boston. "This is the lull before the storm that we're going to have in this country the next decade."

The reason, he said, is that homicides by juveniles as young as 14 or 15 years old are on the rise. They are the leading edge of the mini-baby boom of children in the post-World War II baby boomers, and they haven't yet reached the 18- to 24-year-old age group that traditionally commits the overwhelming majority of murders, he said. "They aren't even there yet, but they're committing homicide," Levin said. "What are they going to do for an encore?"

Former FBI Director Louis Freeh issued a pessimistic statement, saying, "Crime problems are so grave that few Americans will find much comfort in a small reduction in the overall amount of reported crime."

These are the casualties! But why?

In the early '60s, a time when I was in Graduate School, the Highest

Elders in our land decided that God could no longer be mentioned (at least in prayer) in our schools. At that time, he may not have been mentioned very much in our homes either.

What began to happen from about this time on, I believe, were a desensitization of our country's moral sense and a consequent depersonalization of society. We began to become a generation of liars. In 1993, a Gallup Poll, quoted in *Time*, indicated that 96% of Americans admitted to lying on a regular basis.

Satan is the "father of lies." Our Senators and Congressmen lie. Our Presidents and Vice-Presidents lie. Our Elders in the Supreme Court lie. And we don't get too upset about it. In fact, we keep returning them to office because we need them to get what *we* want. Character is not an important factor in many political leaders of our country or among the people who elect them.

Several years ago, I was analyzing the last 30+ years through which I had lived up to that time, while preparing a talk on youth violence. I quickly jotted down some of the lies that I, and most of us, had been affected by and that still dominate today's American culture. Through us, our young people have been affected to a significant degree.

1. God, if he is considered to even exist, is irrelevant to the everyday life of most people.
2. There are no absolutes; everything is relative.
3. Right is what I say it is.
4. My rights come first.
5. Authority is repressive and must be attacked (the 1968 Chicago riots).
6. Freedom is an absolute right (Woodstock).
7. Personal responsibility is passé.
8. If I don't break any laws, it is not immoral (Dr. Kavorkian, Al Gore, Bill Clinton argument).
9. The "System" is the problem.
10. Sex is free - any way I want it.
11. Commitment is unimportant (Live-in and transitory relationships; Rent-a-spouse).
12. Fathers can beget and then forget their kids. Over 50% do.
13. Life is cheap. ("Abort it." "Mercy-kill" it through physician-assisted suicides or otherwise.)
14. Children are a bother. (They restrict our freedom and lifestyle and careers.)
15. I have a right to prevent life from being created through pills, creams, IUDs, condoms, and operations.
16. A fetus is just an intrusive blob of tissue that can be gotten rid of at will and for any reason. (If this is true *before* birth, what makes it

any different *after* birth?)

17. People are expendable (They have a "right" to "die with dignity.")
18. I can have it all (So say the beer commercials and other advertising.)
19. Life is meaningless. Suicide is a "solution" (So sing the Rock stars.) Suicide is now the third leading cause of death among adolescents, after accidents and homicides (Blumenthal, 1990)
20. Parental discipline is defined as child abuse and violence (Justice and Justice, 1990; Susanne Steinmetz and Murray Sraus, 1973).
21. Lawsuits and violence are the ways to resolve conflicts and grievances.
22. "Gay marriage" is my right, and my partner and I can even raise children together.

Here are some of the consequences of those lies:

↳ According to official statistics, approximately 22,500 murders were committed in 1992, as well as 109,062 rapes, 1,126,974 aggravated assaults, and 672,478 robberies (Uniform Crime Report, 1993). Over 68% of the homicides reported in 1992 were committed by people using firearms; over 80% of those homicides involved handguns.

↳ There are over 3 million cohabiting couples in the United States. Cohabitation has been increasing at a rate of about 15% a year for the past decade or more.

↳ According to one study, young, married, childless couples were found to be the happiest of all marital-status groups. Childless marriages were seen to be less stressed and emotionally satisfying. Many young wives do not regard childbearing as necessary to a woman's role (Campbell, 1975).

↳ Almost 68% of American women with children under 18 work outside the home (Statistical Abstract, 1993).

↳ When the wives work out of necessity, marital happiness suffers (Orden & Bradburn, 1970).

↳ As women gain greater economic freedom and independence, couples are more likely to end an unhappy marriage.

↳ A significant proportion of men have found it too hard to adjust to the demand for greater equality or to find wives with more traditional views. Instead, they are choosing to avoid lasting relationships in favor of the single life (Gerson, 1993).

↳ America's divorce rate is the highest in the world. One out of every two marriages ends in divorce; 67% of all second marriages end in divorce (Bureau of Census).

↳ Every 30 seconds, a child's parents divorce (National Center for Health Statistics). Among first marriages, 43% break up within 15 years, about 60% of divorcing couples have kids, and about 1 million children every year experience the divorce of their parents.

- Twenty-four million U.S. children (34% of the total) live in homes without their biological fathers.
- Nearly 20 million children (27%) live in single-parent homes.
- In the year 2000 alone, 1.35 million births (33%) took place out of wedlock.
- About 40% of children living in father-absent homes have not seen their fathers in the past year.
- Children without contact with their biological fathers are on average 2 to 3 times more likely to be poor, use drugs, have educational, health, emotional and behavioral problems, be victims of child abuse, and engage in criminal behavior than are children living with their married, biological or adoptive parents.
- This trend is partially responsible for the significant increase in the proportional female-headed and single-person households in the population.
- 50% of the divorced mothers never receive any child support; 60-80% of the others receive some as ordered.
- One-half of all single mothers are living in poverty; 70% are black; 53% of the whites are Hispanic (Bureau of Census).
- 90% of divorced mothers have custody of their children.
- Single mothers support up to four children on an annual after-tax income of $12,200.
- The biggest single event that takes them out of poverty is remarriage; marriage = economic arrangement, not necessarily a loving relationship.
- Ineffectual restructuring processes drain welfare resources such as AFDC.
- Divorce and desertion are the leading causes of dependence on welfare.
- 60% of all cases in court are domestic relations or domestic relations derived; 25% of judicial time is allotted to these. Each year, between 2,400 and 4,000 are beaten to death by their spouses, and 25% of all female suicides are preceded by a history of battering (Reid, 1991). Between 30% and 40% of the time, a man who abuses his wife also abuses his children (Erlinger, 1987).
- In one study, 65% of abused partners were in live-in (unmarried) situations; 19% were in traditional marriages.

What is the impact on children?

- 1.1 million children are affected annually by divorce (House Select Committee on Children, Youth, and Families, 1987). An estimated 86% of black children and 42% of white children will spend some time in a mother-only or other single-parent household (Bumpass, 1984).
- Ongoing parental conflict is associated with poorer school performance,

22

lower grades, less social competence than peers, more behavioral problems at school, and perceptions of being less intelligent and popular than their classmates (House Select Committee on Children, Youth, and Families - Dr. Neil Kalter).

⇨ Children of divorce are 5 times more likely to be suspended from school, 3 times as likely to need psychological counseling, 2 times as likely to repeat a grade. Children from single-parent families are absent from school more, late to school more often, and show more health problems (Dr. Gene Brody, Study of Competence in Children and Families).

⇨ Divorce is the major etiologic or causal factor in child physical and sexual abuse and neglect.

⇨ 50% or more of non-custodial parents disappear from their child's life (National Institute of Child Health and Human Development).

⇨ 75% of adolescent patients at chemical abuse centers are from single-parent families (Centers for Disease Control, Atlanta, Georgia).

⇨ Every 78 seconds, a child attempts suicide; every 90 minutes, one succeeds (National Center for Health Statistics). Although successful suicide is more common in males than in females, more females attempt suicide (Centers for Disease Control, 1990).

⇨ Every 31 seconds, an adolescent becomes pregnant (National Center for Health Statistics). Teenage women make up about 25% of the population of childbearing age, yet they account for over 45% of all illegitimate births. 70% of teenage pregnancies are single-parent children (Children in Need: Committee for Economic Development).

⇨ 3 out of 5 juveniles in youth correctional facilities are from single-parent families (Bureau of Justice Statistics, 1988). 50% of children on probation are children of divorce.

Scripture speaks of the sins to the third and fourth generation. I believe that we are seeing the casualties of seeds of sins sown back in the "Roaring Twenties." We have had, and continue to have, un-parented children who are trying to parent in a society, and a Church, that doesn't provide the support and encouragement that are needed. We have, raising their children, parents who were infected by the lies of the '60s and '70s.' We are the casualties of our own lies and rebellion.

What do we need? Spiritual warriors, who are sold out to God, their spouses, and their children.

What do our children need? Godly parental role models. Children are conformists, not deviant beyond the normal effects of Original Sin. Their behavior says a lot about their role models.

Children need boundaries. A colt is free to roam and to play at will as long as it stays in the pasture. The fences are put around the pasture to keep the colt from getting hurt in the gullies and on the highways, not to restrict its freedom. Modern trains can run at extremely high speeds as long as they stay on the track or on the rail.

Children need honorable fathers at home. Their healthy psycho-sexual develoment requires it.

Finally, kids need someone to listen and to care. That doesn't mean day-care or pre-school. Their parents should be first in line.

The Wall Street Journal, hardly a Christian publication, has stated that, unless we do something soon to turn our society around, it is going down the drain. Our choice is to continue in our lies and deception or to repent and to prepare for spiritual warfare for our families and for our children. The war is going to be won in the home before it will be won in society or in the Church. We have to decide this day whom we are going to serve -- not with our lips, but with our hearts and with our actions. It is too late to keep playing spiritual games.

Figures from the Children's Defense Fund are from 1989. However, it is safe to conclude that, if anything, the figures are higher today than lower since there doesn't seem to be a moral turnaround in our country at this time.

CAN YOU TAKE ORDERS?
(A Study In Submission)

Jesus, The Model Of Submission

Even as a child, Jesus was the model of submission. When his parents found him in the Temple, Jesus went back with them to Nazareth, where he was obedient to them. (1) He honored his father and mother as one of the Ten Commandments requires.

Throughout his whole ministry Jesus had only one goal: *"I can do nothing on my own...I seek to do not my own will but the will of him who sent me. (2) I have come down from Heaven, not to do my own will but the will of him who sent me. (3) My food is to do the will of him who sent me and to complete his work. (4) Very truly I tell you, the Son can do nothing on his own but only what he sees the Father doing. Whatever the Father does, the Son does likewise."* (5)

When his work was nearing an end, and Jesus was facing his agonizing crucifixion and death, he was still the model of submission: *"My Father, if it is possible, let this cup pass from me; yet not what I want but what you want...if this cannot pass unless I drink it, your will be done."* (6)

"In the days of his flesh, Jesus offered up prayers and supplications with loud cries and tears to the one who was able to save him from death, and he was heard because of his reverent submission. Although he was a Son, he learned obedience through what he suffered." (7) Therefore, when all is completed at the end of time, Christ *"will hand over the kingdom to God the Father, after he has*

destroyed every ruler and every authority and power. When all things are subjected to him, then the Son himself will also be subjected to the one who put all things in subjection under him so that God may be all in all." (8)

The Attitude Of Submission

Submission is a free will action that flows from an attitude. The

25

attitude you should have is the same one that Christ Jesus had! *"Christ was truly God. But, he did not try to remain equal with God. He gave up everything and became a slave, when he became like one of us. Christ was humble. He obeyed God and even died on a Cross. Then, God gave Christ the highest place and honored his Name above all others."* (9)

It is this Jesus who says to you: *"Very truly I tell you, unless a grain of wheat falls into the earth and dies, it remains just a single grain, but if it dies, it bears much fruit. Those who love their life will lose it, and those who hate their life in this world will keep it for eternal life. Whoever serves me must follow me. Where I am, there my servant will be also. The Father will honor whoever serves me.* (10) *So you also, when you have done all that you were ordered to do, say, 'I am a worthless slave; I have done only what I ought to have done!'* (11)

"Remain in me as I remain in you. Just as a branch cannot bear fruit on its own unless it remains on the vine, so neither can you unless you remain in me. Whoever remains in me, and I in him, will bear much fruit because, without me, you can do nothing. (12)

"Truly, unless you change and become like a child, you will never enter the kingdom of Heaven. Whoever becomes humble like a child is the greatest in the kingdom of Heaven. (13) *The greatest among you must become like the youngest, and the leader like one who serves.* (14) *All who exalt themselves will be humbled, and all who humble themselves will be exalted."* (15)

With Christ Jesus as your example, therefore, cleanse yourself *"from every defilement of body and of spirit, making holiness perfect in the fear of God.* (16) *Keep alert, stand firm in your faith, be courageous, be strong. Let all that you do be done in love.* (17) *Be dressed for action and have your lamp lit. Be like those who are waiting for their master to return from a wedding banquet so that they may open the door for him as soon as he comes and knocks.* (18) *He who has the bride is the bridegroom. The friend of the bridegroom, who stands and hears him, rejoices greatly at the bridegroom's voice. He must increase, but you must decrease.* (19)

"Do something to show that you really have given up your sins. (20) *Do all things without murmuring or arguing.* (21) *Stay away, however, from people who are not followers of the Lord! Can someone who is good go along with someone who is evil? Are light and darkness the same? Is Christ a friend of Satan? Can people who follow the Lord have anything in common with those who don't?* (22) *Very truly I tell you, anyone who does not enter the sheepfold by the gate but climbs in by another way is a thief and a bandit.* (23) *We know that God does not listen to sinners but does listen to one who worships him and obeys his will.* (24)

"Who, then, is the faithful and wise slave whom his master has put in charge of his household to give the other slaves their allowance of food at

the proper time? Blessed is that slave whom his master will find at work when he arrives." (25)

Submission To God

Jesus said: *"Not everyone who says to me, 'Lord, Lord,' will enter the kingdom of Heaven but only the one who does the will of my Father in Heaven.* (26) *Whoever does the will of God is my brother and sister and mother.* (27)

"Come to him, a living stone, though rejected by mortals yet chosen and precious in God's sight. (28) *Present your body as a living sacrifice, holy and acceptable to God, which is your spiritual worship. Do not be conformed to this world but be transformed by the renewing of your mind so that you may discern what is the will of God - what is good and acceptable and perfect.* (29)

"You must stop doing anything immoral or evil. Instead, be humble and accept the message that is planted in you to save you. Obey God's message! Do not fool yourself by just listening to it. (30) *Surrender to God! Resist the devil, and he will run from you. Come near to God, and he will come near to you. Clean up your life. Purify your heart. Be humble in God's presence, and he will honor you.* (31)

"Be alert and think straight. Put all your hope in how kind God will be to you when Jesus Christ appears. Behave like an obedient child. Do not let your life be controlled by your desires as it used to be. Always live as God's holy people should because God is the one who chose you, and he is holy. That is why the Scriptures say, 'I am the holy God, and you must be holy too.' (32)

"Love the Lord your God with all your heart, and with all your soul, and with all your strength. (33) *This is the greatest and first commandment.* (34) *The second is this, 'You shall love your neighbor as you love yourself.' There is no other commandment greater than these.* (35) *This is much more important than all whole burnt offerings and sacrifices.* (36)

Finally, *"be patient when you are being corrected! This is how God treats his children. Do not all parents correct their children? God corrects all of his children. If he does not correct you, then you don't really belong to him. Our earthly fathers correct us, and we still respect them. Is it not even better to be given true life by letting your spiritual Father correct you?"* (37)

Submission To Jesus Christ

Jesus said, *"Truly I tell you, whoever does not receive the kingdom of God as a little child will never enter it.* (38) *Anyone who does not honor the Son does not honor the Father who sent him.* (39) *Whoever is not with* me is against me, and whoever does not gather with me scatters. (40) Follow me, and let the dead bury their own dead. (41)

"Come to me, all you who are weary and carrying heavy burdens, and I will give you rest. Take my yoke upon you and learn from me. I am gentle and humble in heart, and you will find rest for your souls. My yoke is easy, and my burden is light. (42)

"If you want to become my follower, deny yourself and take up your cross daily and follow me. (43) Those who want to save their life will lose it, and those who lose their life for my sake will save it. What will it profit them to gain the whole world and forfeit their life? Indeed, what can they give in return for their life? (44)

"Why do you call me 'Lord, Lord,' and do not do what I tell you? I will show you what someone is like who comes to me, hears my words, and acts on them. That one is like a man building a house, who dug deeply and laid the foundation on rock. When a flood arose, the river burst against that house but could not shake it because it had been well built. (45) If you continue in my word, you are truly my disciple. You will know the truth, andthe truth will make you free. (46) If you love me, you will keep my commandments. Those who have my commandments and keep them are those who love me. My Father will love those who love me, and I will love them and reveal myself to them. (47)

"Whoever does the will of God is my brother and sister and mother. (48) Whoever comes to me and does not hate father and mother, wife and children, brothers and sisters, yes, and even life itself, cannot be my disciple. Whoever does not carry the cross and follow me cannot be my disciple. (49) I repeat, whoever loves father or mother more than me is not worthy of me. Whoever loves son or daughter more than me is not worthy of me. Whoever does not take up the cross and follow me is not worthy of me. Those who find their life will lose it, and those who lose their life for my sake will find it. (50) So, therefore, you cannot become my disciple if you do not give up all your possessions. (51)

"Truly I tell you, there is no one who has left house or brothers or sisters or mother or father or children or fields for my sake and for the sake of the good news, who will not receive a hundredfold now in this age -- houses, brothers and sisters, mothers and children, and fields with persecutions -- and, in the age to come, eternal life. But, many who are first will be last, and the last will be first." (52)

Submission In Marriage

"Let marriage be held in honor by all, and let the marriage bed be kept undefiled because God will judge fornicators and adulterers. (53)

"Each of you should love his wife as himself, and a wife should respect her husband. (54) The husband should give to his wife her conjugal rights, and likewise the wife to her husband. The wife does not have authority over her own body, but the husband does; likewise the husband does not have authority over his own body, but the wife does. Do not deprive one another except perhaps by agreement for a set time to devote yourselves to prayer, and then come together again so that Satan may not tempt you because of your lack of self-control. (55)

"Husband, love your wife and never treat her harshly. (56) Love your wife, just as Christ loved the Church and gave himself up for her. (57) Control your own body in holiness and honor, not with lustful passion like those who do not know God. (58) In the same way, show consideration for your wife in your life together, paying honor to the woman as the weaker sex, since she too is an heir of the gracious gift of life -- that you might inherit a blessing. (59)

"Wife, be subject to your husband as is fitting in the Lord. (60) Be subject to your husband as you are to the Lord. The husband is the head of the wife just as Christ is the Head of the Church, the Body of which he is the Savior. Just as the Church is subject to Christ, so also wives ought to be in everything to their husbands. (61) In the same way, accept the authority of your husband so that, even if he does not obey the word, he may be won over without a word by your conduct, when he sees the purity and reverence of your life." (62)

Submission In The Family

"Child, obey your parents in everything because this is your acceptable duty in the Lord. (63) 'Honor your father and mother' -- this is the first commandment with a promise: 'so that it may be well with you and you may live long on the earth.' (64)

"Parents, do not provoke your children so they may not become discouraged. (65) Do not provoke your children to anger but bring them up in the discipline and instruction of the Lord." (66)

Submission In Christian Service

"Be subject to one another out of reverence for Christ. (67) What I am saying is for your own good -- it isn't to limit your freedom. I want to help you to live right and to love the Lord above all else. (68) Therefore *"be steadfast, immovable, always excelling in the work of the Lord because you know that, in the Lord, your labor is not in vain."* (69)

Submission To Religious Authority

"The Pharisees and the teachers of the Law are experts in the Law of Moses," Jesus told his followers. "So, obey everything they teach you but do not do as they do. After all, they say one thing and do something else." (70) Jesus is establishing a principle here that applies as well to all authority, such as civil and parental authority, namely, that God's authority is placed in the *offices* that he establishes over his people. Therefore, the persons who hold these offices or positions, whether properly or by their own power, *by that fact* possess the authority that goes with that office. They will be held accountable to God for how they exercise that authority.

Some take these offices upon themselves for selfish or other illegitimate reasons. Thus, their lives may not measure up to God's standards for those in authority. However, God places the authority they do exercise there, and you are to submit to it, unless it concerns something illegal or immoral. You are to discern carefully what they teach and obey that teaching that is in line with the teachings of God and of his Son, Jesus Christ. But, you are not to imitate their actions when they do not, in their own personal lives, practice what they preach.

You are also, to the degree that you have the option, to be careful under whose authority, especially religious, that you place yourself. You should withdraw from that authority that is not being exercised properly, even if this means changing churches or jobs.

Submission To Civil Authority

"Obey the rulers who have authority over you. Only God can give authority to anyone, and he puts these rulers in their places of power. People who oppose the authorities are opposing what God has done, and will be punished. Rulers are a threat to evil people, not to good people. There is no need to be afraid of the authorities. Just do right, and they will praise you for it. After all, they are God's servants, and it is their duty to help you.

"If you do something wrong, you ought to be afraid because these rulers have the right to punish you. They are God's servants to punish criminals to show how angry God is. But, you should obey the rulers because you know it is the right thing to do and not just because of God's anger.

"You must also pay your taxes. The authorities are God's servants, and it is their duty to take care of these matters. Pay all that you owe, whether it is taxes and fees or respect and honor. (71) *Give to the (authority) the things that are the (authority's), and to God the things that are God's.* (72)

"For the Lord's sake, accept the authority of every human

institution, whether of the (authority) as supreme, or of governors, as sent by him to punish those who do wrong and to praise those who do right. It is God's will that, by doing right, you should silence the ignorance of the foolish. As a servant of God, live as one who is free but do not use your freedom as a pretext for evil. Honor everyone. Love the family of believers. Fear God. Honor the (authority). (73) Be subject to rulers and authorities, be obedient, be ready for every good work, speak evil of no one, avoid quarreling, be gentle, and show every courtesy to everyone." (74)

Submission To Other Authority

"Obey those over you and do what they say. They are watching over you and must answer to God. So, do not make them sad as they do their work. Make them happy. Otherwise, they will not be able to help you at all. (75)

Remember what Jesus said: *"Very truly I tell you, whoever receives one whom I send receives me; whoever receives me receives him who sent me. (76) Whoever listens to you listens to me, whoever rejects you rejects me, and whoever rejects me rejects the one who sent me. (77)*

"Are students better than their teacher? But, when they are fully trained, they will be like their teacher. (78) A disciple is not above the teacher, nor a slave above the master. It is enough for the disciple to be like the teacher, and the slave like the master. (79)

"Those who are under (employment) must regard (those over them) as worthy of full respect so that the Name of God and our teaching may not suffer abuse. (80) (Employees) are to be under the control of (those over them) in all respects, giving them satisfaction, not talking back to them or stealing from them but exhibiting complete good faith so as to adorn the doctrine of God our Savior in every way. (81)

"Accept the authority of (those over you) with all deference, not only those who are kind and gentle but also those who are harsh. It is a credit to you if, being aware of God, you endure pain while suffering unjustly. (82) Obey (those over you) with fear and trembling, in singleness of heart, as you obey Christ; not only while being watched, and in order to please them, but as slaves of Christ, doing the will of God from the heart. Render service with enthusiasm as to the Lord and not to people, knowing that whatever good you do, you will receive the same again from the Lord, whether you are a slave or free. (83) Whatever your task, put yourself into it as done for the Lord and not for (those over you) since you know that from the Lord you will receive the inheritance as your reward. Be a slave of the Lord Christ. (84)

"Those who have believing masters must not be disrespectful to them on the ground that they are members of the Church. Rather, they must

serve them all the more since those who benefit by their service are believers and are beloved." (85)

Submission To One Another

Jesus said, *"I give you a new commandment, that you love one another. Just as I have loved you, you also should love one another. By this, everyone will know that you are my disciples, if you have love for one another. (86) If I, your Lord and Teacher, have washed your feet, you also ought to wash one another's feet. I have set you an example that you also should do as I have done to you. Very truly I tell you, servants are not greater than their master or messengers greater than the one who sent them. (87)*

"Whoever wants to be great among you must be your servant, and whoever wishes to be first among you must be your slave, just as the Son of Man came not to be served but to serve and to give his life a ransom for many. (88) The greatest among you must become like the youngest, and the leader like one who serves. (89)

"(Employers), do the same. Stop threatening. (90) Treat your (employees) justly and fairly (91) because you know that both of you have the same Master in Heaven, and with him there is no partiality. (92)

"In the same way, you who are younger must accept the authority of those who are older. All of you must clothe yourselves with humility in your dealings with one another because 'God opposes the proud but gives grace to the humble.' (93)

"Be subject to one another out of reverence for Christ. (94) Live a life worthy of the calling to which you have been called, with all humility and gentleness, with patience, bearing with one another

in love, making every effort to maintain the unity of the Spirit in the bond of peace. (95)

"Owe no one anything except to love one another for the one who loves another has fulfilled the law. (96) You were called to freedom. Do not use your freedom as an opportunity for self-indulgence but, through love, become slaves to one another. The whole law is summed up in a single commandment, 'Love your neighbor as yourself.' If, however, you bite and devour one another, take care that you are not consumed by one another. (97)

"As in one body we have many members, and not all the members have the same function, so we who are many are one Body in Christ. Individually, we are members one of another. We have gifts that differ according to the grace given to us: prophecy, in proportion to faith; ministry, in ministering; the teacher, in teaching; the exhorter, in exhortation; the giver, in generosity; the leader, in diligence; the

32

compassionate, in cheerfulness.

"Let love be genuine: hate what is evil, hold fast to what is good, love one another with mutual affection, outdo one another in showing honor. Do not lag in zeal, be ardent in spirit, and serve the Lord. Rejoice in hope, be patient in suffering, persevere in prayer. Contribute to the needs of the saints and extend hospitality to strangers. (98)

"Pass judgment on one another no longer but resolve instead never to put a stumbling block or hindrance in the way of another. (99) *Do nothing from selfish ambition or conceit but, in humility, regard others as better than yourselves. Let each of you look not to your own interests but to the interests of others.* (100)

Give to everyone who begs from you and do not refuse anyone who wants to borrow from you. (101)

"Bless those who persecute you; bless and do not curse them. Rejoice with those who rejoice, weep with those who weep. Live in harmony with one another. Do not be haughty but associate with the lowly. Do not claim to be wiser than you are. Do not repay anyone evil for evil but take thought for what is noble in the sight of all. If it is possible, so far as it depends on you, live peaceably with all.

"Beloved, never avenge yourselves but leave room for the wrath of God for it is written, 'Vengeance is mine, I will repay, says the Lord.' Rather, 'if your enemies are hungry, feed them. If they are thirsty, give them something to drink. By doing this, you will heap burning coals on their heads. Do not be overcome by evil but overcome evil with good. (102)

"I say to you that listen, love your enemies, do good to those who hate you, bless those who curse you, pray for those who abuse you. Give to everyone who begs from you and, if anyone takes away your goods, do not ask for them again. Do to others as you would have them do to you. (103)

"Let us then pursue what makes for peace and for mutual up building. (104) *We who are strong ought to put up with the failings of the weak and not to please ourselves. Each of us must please our neighbor for the good purpose of building up the neighbor.* (105)

"Admonish the idlers, encourage the faint hearted, help the weak, be patient with all of them. See that none of you repays evil for evil but always seeks to do good to one another and to all. Rejoice always, pray without ceasing, and give thanks in all circumstances because this is the will of God in Christ Jesus for you. " (106)

(1)	Luke 2:51	(33)	Deuteronomy 6:5
(2)	John 5:30b	(34)	Matthew 22:38
(3)	John 6:38	(35)	Mark 12:31
(4)	John 4:34	(36)	Mark 12:33b
(5)	John 5:19	(37)	Hebrews 12:7-9

(6)   Matthew 26:39, 42

(7)   Hebrews 5:7 & 8

(8)   1 Corinthians 15:24, 28

(9)   Philippians 2:5-9

(10) John 12:24-26

(11) Luke 17: 9 & 10

(12) John 15:4, 5b

(13) Matthew 18:3 & 4

(14) Luke 22:26

(15) Matthew 18:3 & 4

(16) 2 Corinthians 7:1

(17) 1 Corinthians 16: 13-14

(18) Luke 12:35-36

(19) John 3:29-30

(20) Luke 3:8

(21) Philippians 2:14

(22) 2 Corinthians 6: 14-15

(23) John 10:1

(24) John 9:31

(25) Matthew 24:46-47

(26) Matthew 7:21

(27) Mark 3:35

(28) 1 Peter 2:4

(29) Romans 12:1b-2

(30) James 1:21-22

(31) James 4:7-8a, 10

(32) 1 Peter 1:13-16

(38)   Mark 10:15

(39)   John 5:23b

(40)   Matthew 12:30

(41)   Matthew 8:22

(42)   Matthew 11:28-30

(43)   Matthew 16:23

(44)   Matthew 16:25 & 26

(45)   Luke 6:46-48

(46)   John 8:31 & 32

(47)   John 14:15, 21

(48)   Mark 3:50

(49)   Luke 14:26 & 27

(50)   Matthew10:37

(51)   Luke 14:33

(52)   Mark 10:37

(53)

(54)   Ephesians 5:33

(55)   1 Corinthians 7:3-5

(56)   Colossians 3:19

(57)   Ephesians 5:28

(58)   1 Thessalonians 4:3

(59)   1 Peter 3:7

(60)   Colossians 3:18

(61)   Ephesians 5:21-24

(62)   1 Peter 3:1 & 2

(63)   Colossians 3:20

(64)   Ephesians 6:2 & 3

(65)   Colossians 5:21

(66)   Ephesians 6:4

(67)   Ephesians 5:21

(68)   1 Corinthians 7:35

(69)   1 Corinthians 15:58

(70)   Matthew 23: 2 & 3

(71)   Romans 13:1-7

(72)   Matthew 22:21b

(73)   1 Peter 3:13-17

(74)   Titus 3:1 & 2

(75)   Hebrews 13:17

(76)   John 13:20

(77)   Luke 10:16

(78)   Luke 5:40

(79)   Matthew 10:24 & 25

(80)   1 Timothy 6:1

(88)   Matthew 20:26b-28

(89)   Luke 22:26

(90)   Ephesians 6:8a

(91)   Colossians 4:1a

(92)   Ephesians 6:8b

(93)   1 Peter 5:5

(94)   Ephesians 5:21

(95)   Ephesians 4:1-3

(96)   Romans 13:8

(97)   Galatians 5:13-15

(98)   Romans 12:4-13

(99)   Romans 14:13

(100) Philippians 2:3 & 4

(81) Titus 9 & 10
(82) 1 Peter 2: 18 & 19
(83) Ephesians 6:5-8
(84) Colossians 3:23
(85) 1 Timothy 6:2
(86) John 13:34 & 35
(87) John 13:14-16

(101) Matthew 4:32
(102) Romans 12:14-21
(103) Luke 6:27-31
(104) Romans 14:19
(105) Romans 15:1 & 2
(106) 1 Thessalonians 5: 14-18

BY WHOSE AUTHORITY?
(A Look At Authority)

The Nature And Source Of Authority

Authority relates to an Author or Source, not to an ability or power. The word comes from the Greek EXOUSIA. Ex denotes origin; ousia = substance. The word *power* comes from the Greek DUNAMAI (verb) or DUNAMIS (noun), meaning *to be able* as a verb, or *ability, force, might*, as a noun. From this comes the word dynamite. Power is the *ability* to do something or to keep it from being done; authority is the *right* to do something. Someone can have authority without power or power without authority.

As always, Jesus Christ reveals the true source of all authority. Jesus knew that *"the Father had given all things into his hands and that he had come from God and was going to God. "* (1) *"I came from God and now I am here,"* he said. *"I did not come on my own, but he sent me. (2) You know me and know where I am from. I have not come on my own. But, the one who sent me is true, and you do not know him. I know him because I am from him, and he sent me. (3)*

"I have come in my Father's Name. (4) I have not spoken on my own, but the Father who sent me has himself given me a commandment about what to say and what to speak. I know that his commandment is eternal life. What I speak, therefore, I speak just as the Father has told me. (5)

"Just as the Father has life in himself, so he has granted the Son also to have life in himself and has given him authority to execute judgment because he is the Son of Man. (6) Indeed just as the Father raises the dead and gives them life, so also the Son gives life to whomever he wishes. The

Father judges no one but has given all judgment to the Son so that all may honor the Son just as they honor the Father. Anyone who does not honor the Son does not honor the Father who sent him. (7)

"The works that the Father has given me to complete, the very works that I am doing, testify on my behalf that the Father has sent me. (8) The works that I do in my Father's Name testify to me." (9)

In order that we might know that Jesus was speaking the truth, the Father himself put his stamp of approval on him. *"When Jesus had been baptized, just as he came up from the water, suddenly the heavens were opened to him and he saw the Spirit of God descending like a dove and alighting on him. A voice from Heaven said, 'This is my beloved Son with whom I am well pleased."* (10) The Father further confirmed the work of Jesus by raising him from death.

Truly, then, *"the kingdom of the world has become the kingdom of our Lord and of his Messiah, and he shall reign forever and ever."* (11) The father gave him *"authority over all people to give eternal life to all whom (the Father has) given him."* (12)

The Authority Of Jesus - Its Extents And Limits

Jesus said, *"When you have lifted up the Son of Man, then you will realize that I AM and that I do nothing on my own but speak these things as the Father instructed me. The one who sent me is with me. He has not left me alone because I always do what is pleasing to him.* (13)

"The one who comes from Heaven is above all. He testifies to what he has seen and heard, yet no one accepts his testimony. He whom God has sent speaks the words of God for he gives the Spirit without measure. The Father loves the Son and has placed all things in his hands. (14) All authority in Heaven and on earth has been given to me. (15) The Son can do nothing on his own but only what he sees the Father doing. Whatever the Father does, the Son does likewise. The Father loves the Son and shows him all that he himself is doing. (16)

"I can do nothing on my own. As I hear, I judge, and my judgment is just because I seek to do not my own will but the will of him who sent me. (17) My teaching is not mine but his who sent me. Anyone who resolves to do the will of God will know whether my teaching is from God or whether I am speaking on my own. Those who speak on their own seek their own glory, but the one who seeks the glory of him who sent him is true, and there is nothing false in him. (18)

"To sit at my right hand and at my left, this is not mine to grant. It is for those for whom my Father has prepared it. (19) It is not for you to know the times or periods that the Father has set by his own authority. (20)

"I lay down my life in order to take it up again. No one takes it from

me, but I lay it down of my own accord. I have power to lay it down, and I have power to take it up again. I have received this command from my Father. (21) I am the first and the last and the living one. I was dead and see: I am alive forever and ever. I have the keys of Death and of Hades (*Hell*). (22)

> "*Everything that the Father gives me will come to me. Anyone who comes to me I will never drive away because I have come down from Heaven not to do my own will but the will of him who sent me.*" (23)

It Extends To His Teaching

The people "*were astounded at his teaching, for he taught them as one having authority, not as the scribes.*" (24)

It Extends To Sin

"*When Jesus saw their faith, he said to the paralytic, 'Take heart, son; your sins are forgiven.' Then some of the scribes said to themselves, 'This man is blaspheming.' But, Jesus, perceiving their thoughts, said, 'Why do you think evil in your hearts? Which is easier, to say, 'Your sins are forgiven,' or to say, 'Stand up, take your bed and go to your home.' The paralytic stood up and went to his home. When the crowds saw it, they were filled with awe and glorified God, who had given such authority to human beings.*" (25)

It Extends To Physical And Spiritual Sickness

"*Jesus went throughout Galilee, teaching in their synagogues, proclaiming the good news of the kingdom, and curing every disease and every sickness among the people. His fame spread throughout all Syria, and they brought to him all the sick, those who were afflicted with various diseases and pains, demoniacs, epileptics, and paralytics, and he cured them. (26) Wherever he went, into villages or cities or farms, they laid the sick in the marketplaces and begged him that they might touch even the fringe of his cloak. All who touched it were healed. (27)*

"They brought to him many who were possessed with demons, and he cast out the spirits with a word and cured all who were sick. (28) He cured many who were sick with various diseases and cast out many demons but would not permit the demons to speak because they knew him. (29)

"Jesus cured many people of diseases, plagues, and evil spirits and had given sight to many who were blind. (30) The people 'were astounded beyond measure, saying, "He has done everything well; he even makes the deaf to hear and the mute to speak. (31) With authority and power he

commands the unclean spirits, and out they come.' " (32)

It Extends To All Creation

"Taking the five loaves and the two fishes, he looked up to Heaven, blessed and broke the loaves, and gave them to his disciples to set before the people. He divided the two fish among them all, and all ate and were filled." (33)

On other occasions, Jesus likewise fed the crowd. Once, when a great windstorm arose, and the waves beat into the boat so that the boat was being swamped, Jesus was asleep in the stern. *"He woke up, rebuked the wind, and said to the sea, 'Peace! Be still!' Then, the wind ceased, and there was a dead calm."* (34) The disciples *"were filled with great awe and said to one another, 'Who is this that even the wind and the sea obey him?' "* (35)

It Extends To The Sabbath

"Then he said to them, 'The Sabbath was made for mankind, not mankind for the Sabbath, so the Son of Man is lord, even of the Sabbath." (36)

It Is Always Effective

The authority of Jesus extends, as we have seen, to physical sickness and spiritual oppression. It requires only a touch or a word from Jesus to be effective. There are no magical rituals or even sacrifices. His authority comes from being himself the sacrificial Lamb who *"took our infirmities and bore our diseases."* (37)

His authority comes also from putting the will of his Father first. Obedience to the Father first was the key to the authority of Jesus. Thus, he has the very authority of God on earth even to forgive sins.

The authority of Jesus is limitless, extending to the physical and spiritual worlds. It is so powerful that it requires only a touch, a word, and an invitation to share in it.

Its Delegation To His Followers

The Nature Of Delegated Authority

All authority under God is delegated authority. Delegated authority is exercised in the name of the Author and cannot be exercised properly apart from the Author. Moreover the exercise of authority demands accountability to the Author.

Jesus desires and pleads for others with whom he can share his authority. The only purpose for his authority on earth is to help and to save those who are worried and helpless, like sheep without a shepherd.

Compassion and pity, not power, are what trigger the authority of Jesus. He commands us to pray for workers with the same pity and compassion for his people so that he can share his authority over sickness, death, sin, and even spiritual forces that oppress his people, hold them in bondage, and keep them from enjoying the freedom of children of God that he desires for each person.

The authority of Jesus liberates; man's authority often dominates. He desires to set people free in him.

Delegation First To The Apostles

Jesus called to himself the men he wanted. They came to him, and he chose twelve *"to be with him, to be sent out to proclaim the message, and to have authority to cast out demons. (38)*

"He called the twelve and began to send them out two by two. (39) He gave them authority over unclean spirits, to cast them out, and to cure every disease and every sickness. (40)

"I confer on you, just as my Father has conferred on me, a kingdom. (41) As the Father has sent me, so I send you," Jesus said. *"When he had said this, he breathed on them and said to them, 'Receive the Holy Spirit. If you forgive the sins of any, they are forgiven them; if you retain the sins of any, they are retained. (42)*

"Go into all the world and proclaim the good news to the whole creation. The one who believes and is baptized will be saved, but the one who does not believe will be condemned. (43) All authority in Heaven and on earth has been given to me. Go and make disciples of all nations, baptizing them in the Name of the Father and of the Son and of the Holy Spirit and teaching them to obey everything that I have commanded you. And, remember, I am with you always, to the end of the age." (44)

Delegation To The Seventy-Two

"The Lord appointed seventy-two others and sent them on ahead of him in pairs to every town and place where he himself intended to go. (45) Jesus said, *'I have given you authority to tread on snakes and scorpions and over all the power of the enemy, and nothing will hurt you.' "* (46)

Delegation To All Who Follow Him

"These signs will accompany those who believe: by using my Name

they will cast out demons. They will speak with new tongues. They will pick up snakes, and, if they drink any deadly thing, it will not hurt them. They will lay their hands on the sick, and they will recover. (47)

"To everyone who conquers and continues to do my works to the end, I will give authority over the nations to rule them with an iron rod, as when clay pots are shattered, even as I also received authority from my Father. To the one who conquers, I will also give the morning star. (48)

"To the one who conquers, I will give a place with me on my throne, just as I myself conquered and sat down with my Father on his throne. (49)

"Truly I tell you, whatever you bind on earth will be bound in Heaven, and whatever you loose on earth will be loosed in Heaven. Again, truly I tell you, if two of you agree on earth about anything you ask, it will be done for you by my Father in Heaven. Where two or three are gathered in my Name, I am there among them. (50)

"God did not subject the coming world to angels. But, someone has testified somewhere (Psalm 8), 'What are human beings that you are mindful of them, or mortals, that you care for them? You have made them for a little while lower than the angels. You have crowned them with glory and honor, subjecting all things under their feet.'

"Now in subjecting all things to them, God left nothing outside of their control. As it is, we do not yet see everything in subjection to them, but we do see Jesus, who for a little while was made lower than the angels, now crowned with glory and honor because of the suffering of death so that, by the grace of God, he might taste death for everyone." (51)

The authority that God has given to you is authority to build up, not to tear down. (52) When you really trust that Jesus has the authority of God, the Father, over and in all things, you will be able to ask for anything or intercede for anyone and know that you will be heard. This faith is what brings you into the Kingdom, nothing else.

Its Expression In Service

Jesus called the twelve to him and said, *"You know that the rulers of the Gentiles lord it over them, and their great ones are tyrants over them. It will not be so among you. Whoever wishes to be great among you must be your servant, and whoever wishes to be first among you must be your slave, just as the Son of Man came not to be served but to serve and to give his life a ransom for many.* (53)

Civil Authority

Pilate said to Jesus, *" 'Do you refuse to speak to me? Do you not know that I have power to release you and power to crucify you?' Jesus answered, 'You would have no power over me unless it had been given to you from above.'* (54)

> *"There is no authority except from God, and those authorities that exist have been instituted by God. Therefore, whoever resists authority resists what God has appointed, and those who resist will incur judgment because it is God's servant for our good. It is the servant of God to execute wrath on the wrongdoer. For the same reason, you also pay taxes because the authorities are God's servants, busy with this very thing. Pay to them all what is due them--taxes to whom taxes are due, revenue to whom revenue is due, respect to whom respect is due, honor to whom honor is due."* (55)

Religious Authority

> *"Jesus said to the crowds and to his disciples, 'The scribes and the Pharisees sit on Moses' seat. Therefore, do whatever they teach you and follow it but do not do as they do because they do not practice what they teach.' "* (56)

A subtle distinction is made here between what religious authorities *say* and what they *do*. To the extent that they teach and preach the authentic Word of God, their authority is to be respected, and they are to be obeyed because their authority exists in the office they hold. However, where their own example is contrary to what they teach or preach, they are not to be imitated.

The Authority Of Satan

Whether we like it or not, Satan or the Devil is the present legitimate ruler of this world. Authority over all creation was originally given to human beings in the Garden of Eden. God's plan was for them to use and to rule over creation under him. But, when Adam and Eve yielded to Satan's deception instead of God's truth, they also yielded their authority to another creature. Thus even though Satan stole man's authority by deception, in effect he now has it, unless you reclaim it through Jesus Christ who, as man, overcame Satan's kingdom through his death, resurrection, and ascension. Jesus has now, in his humanity, defeated Satan and destroyed his authority. Unless you have chosen to submit to the Lordship of and authority of Jesus, you are still under Satan's dominion and authority.

So it is that, when Satan led Jesus up and showed him, in an instant, all the kingdoms of the world, he was truthfully able to say, *"To you I will give their glory and all this authority because it has been given over to me, and I give it to anyone I please. If you, then, will worship me, it will all be yours."* (57)

Obedience to Jesus is the key to your authority over Satan, as

42

obedience to the Father first of all was the key to the authority of Jesus.

The Exercise Of Authority

A brief word must be said here about the proper exercise of authority. It is one thing to *have* authority and another thing to *exercise* it. A policeman, for instance, has authority when he is on duty but cannot exercise his authority any way and any time he desires. The exercise of authority, like the authority itself, is under the direction of and in accordance with the will of the Author.

Jesus again gave us the example of the proper exercise of authority when he said that he only said what he heard the Father saying and did what he saw the Father doing. The key once again is to remember and to recognize where your authority comes from and to whom you are accountable for its use. The authority you exercise as a Christian is always in the Name of (that is, in the Person of) Jesus. You cannot properly exercise your authority apart from Jesus.

Having said that, however, most of us do not have a problem exercising our authority improperly. Our tendency is to fail to use it at all! If you fail to use the power of the Holy Spirit with which you have been baptized, you are really no better off than those who have not been baptized at all!

Failure to use your authority not only will hinder the work Jesus gave you to do but also will encourage Satan to use his authority against you and against the Kingdom of God.

(1) John 13:3
(2) John 8:42b
(3) John 7:28-29
(4) John 5:43
(5) John 12:49-50
(6) John 5:26-27
(7) John 5:21
(8) John 5:36b
(9) John 11:25b
(10) Matthew 3:16 & 17
(11) Revelation 11:15
(12) John 17:2
(13) John 8:28
(14) John 3:31b-32, 34-35
(15) Matthew 28:18
(16) John 5:19-20

(26) Matthew 4:23
(27) Mark 6:5-6
(28) Matthew 8:16
(29) Mark 1:34
(30) Luke 7L21
(31) Mark 7:37
(32) Luke 4:36b
(33) Mark 6:41
(34) Mark 4:39
(35) Mark 4:41
(36) Mark 2:27-28
(37) Matthew 8:17
(38) Mark 3:13-15
(39) Mark 6:7
(40) Matthew 10:1-5
(41) Luke 22:29
(42) John 20:21-23

LOYALTY TO YOUR UNIT

Loyalty To The Lord

How many times have we not read throughout the Bible, seen in the history of the Church, and witnessed all around us even today the Lord saying something like the following? *"I brought you up from Egypt and brought you into the land that I had promised to your ancestors. I said, 'I will never break my covenant with you. For your part, do not make a covenant with the inhabitants if this land; tear down their altars.' But, you have not obeyed my command. See what you have done! So now I say, I will not drive them out before you, but they will become adversaries to you, and their gods shall be a snare to you."* (1)

Sure enough, *"The people served the Lord during the entire lifetime of Joshua and of those elders who outlived Joshua and who had seen all the great work which the Lord had done for Israel. But, once the rest of that generation were gathered to their fathers, and a later generation arose that did not know the Lord or what he had done for Israel, the Israelites offended the Lord by serving the Baals. Abandoning the Lord, the God of their fathers, who had led them out of the land of Egypt, they followed the other gods of the various nations around them and, by their worship of these gods, provoked the Lord.*

"Because they had thus abandoned him and served Baal and the Ashtaroth, the anger of the Lord flared up against Israel, and he delivered them over to plunderers who despoiled them. He allowed them to fall into the power of their enemies around about, whom they were no longer able to withstand. Whatever they undertook, the Lord turned into disaster for them, as, in his warning, he had sworn he would do, till they were in great distress.

45

"Even when the Lord raised up judges to deliver them from the power of their despoilers, they did not listen to their judges but abandoned themselves to the worship of other gods. They were quick to stray from the way their fathers had taken and did not follow their example of obedience to the commandments of the Lord.

"Whenever the Lord raised up judges for them, he would be with the judge and save them from the power of their enemies as long as the judge lived. It was thus the Lord took pity on their distressful cries of affliction under their oppressors. But, when the judge died, they would relapse and do worse than their fathers, following other gods in service and worship, relinquishing none of their evil practices or stubborn conduct." (2)

You need to examine your own loyalty to the Lord God. May it not be said of you, *"Many proclaim themselves loyal, but who can find one worthy of trust?"* (3)

Jesus says even this day, "My heart is still the heart that comes to seek and to save the lost, and so I would have you, my people, come to know the kindness of my heart. If the world around you is to know my kindness, is it not necessary for you, my people, to turn from self-centeredness, to turn from self-security, from the fears of rejection, from your own rebellion? How will the world know my kindness if your hearts are yet in bondage? Therefore, I desire to draw you into my heart so that you may willingly and freely shed the garments of your old ways and that my heart and your heart may beat as one." (4)

Loyalty To Yourself

The next most important area of loyalty is to yourself. *"My child, with humility have self-esteem; prize yourself as you deserve. Who will acquit him who condemns himself? Who will honor him who discredits himself?"* (5)

Loyalty To Your Spouse

Many today are talking about *their* ministry. People are going here and there and everywhere "doing something for the Lord." Husband, the Lord has been saying it over and over in our day, so let's get it settled -- after your ministry to the Lord in praise and worship and then to yourself, your first and most important ministry is to your wife! Before any other ministry, before any other work. Wife, your first and most important ministry is to your husband and to your children, if you have any. Before a job outside the home, before a career, before a ministry in a church. Anything else is just plain out of order, and God cannot and will not bless it.

Loyalty to your wife means protecting and defending her from attack from any source, even – and sometimes, unfortunately, *especially* -- from your brothers and sisters in the Lord! If someone sees something in your wife that needs to be corrected, it is his or her obligation to tell you, not her. A man should not counsel your wife while you are not present or unless you have given permission unless, of course, you are guilty of abusing or sinning against her in some way. You are the spiritual head, the covering of your wife. Be loyal to her!

In this regard Deuteronomy gives a principle that the Church would do well to heed in calling men into ministries that entail a lot of time and responsibility: *"When a man is newly wed, he need not go out on a military expedition, nor shall any public duty be imposed on him. He shall be exempt for one year for the sake of his family, to bring joy to the wife he has married."* (6) Newlyweds, whether in ministry or not, need time to get their primary relationship with each other established. The Church needs to respect that need!

Loyalty To Your Children

Father, are you really loyal enough to your children to spend time with them, to care about what is going on with them, or to discipline them the way they need to be, or are you again more loyal to your job or ministry?

You are the spiritual leader of your church home. Paul tells Timothy, a Church leader *"must manage his own household well, keeping his children submissive and respectful in every way because, if someone does not know how to manage his own household, how can he take care of God's Church."* (7)

Loyalty To The Family

By family here, I mean both your blood family and your spiritual family.

In the Book of Numbers, we read the story of a family that was both: *"While they were at Hazeroth, Miriam and Aaron (Moses' brother and sister) spoke against Moses because of the Cushite women whom he has married and said, 'Has the Lord spoken only through Moses? Has he not spoken through us also?' And the Lord heard it. Now, the man Moses was very humble, more so than anyone else on the face of the earth. Suddenly, the Lord said to Moses, Aaron, and Miriam, 'Come out, you three, to the tent of meeting.' So, the three of them came out. Then, the Lord came down in a pillar of cloud, stood at the entrance of the tent, and called Aaron and Miriam, and they both came forward. He said, 'Hear my words: When there are prophets among you, I the Lord make myself known to them in visions; I speak to them in dreams. Not so with my servant Moses. He is entrusted* with my entire house. With him, I speak face to face--clearly, not in riddles; and he beholds the form of the Lord. Why, then, were you not afraid to speak against my servant Moses?' The anger of the Lord was kindled against them, and he departed.

"When the cloud went away from over the tent, Miriam had become leprous, as white as snow. Aaron turned towards Miriam and saw that she was leprous. Then, Aaron said to Moses, 'Oh, my lord, do not punish us for a sin that we have so foolishly committed. Do not let her be like one stillborn, whose flesh is half consumed when it comes out of its mother's womb.' Moses cried to the Lord, 'O God, please heal her.' But, the Lord said to Moses, 'If her father had but spit in her face, would she not bear her shame for seven days? Let her be shut out of the camp for seven days. After that, she may be brought in again. So, Miriam was shut out of the camp for seven days. The people did not set out on the march until Miriam had been brought in again." (8)

The Lord frowns upon sibling rivalry in any form, but especially when those whom he has chosen are attacked.

Jesus has spoken to us again in our day about loyalty to one another in the Family of God --whether we are Pentecostal, Baptist, Presbyterian, Catholic, Orthodox, non-denominational, or whatever: "I am not pleased with the state of my Church, the condition of my people. There is suspicion and hostility among you. There is argumentativeness among you. Some of you are still more committed to your friends and neighbors and your acquaintances than you are to my people, to those who bear my Name. It is important that you repent. It is important that you turn away from all those sins that keep you separated from your brothers and sisters. Now is the time for you to turn away from these things. I will give you the understanding and the strength that you need to be one people." (9)

Loyalty To Civil Authority

A final area the Lord wants to call you to loyalty to is the area of civil obedience and responsibility. Scripture again gives us some examples to follow: "Darius decided to appoint over his entire kingdom one hundred and twenty satraps to safeguard his interests. These were accountable to three supervisors, one of whom was Daniel. Daniel outshone all the supervisors and satraps because an extraordinary spirit was in him, and the king thought of giving him authority over the entire kingdom. Therefore, the supervisors and satraps tried to find grounds for accusation against Daniel as regards the administration. But, they could accuse him of no wrongdoing; because he was trustworthy, no fault of neglect or misconduct was to be found in him. Then, these men said to themselves, 'We shall find no grounds for accusation against this Daniel unless by way of the law of *his God.' "* (10) If this cannot be said about you, the Lord has much to teach you about loyalty to your country and to your civil leaders!

How about David? *"The king sent a summons to Ahimelech the priest, son of Ahitub, and to all his family who were priests in Nob, and they all came to the king. Then, Saul said, 'Listen, son of Ahitub!' He replied, 'Yes, my lord.' Saul asked him, 'Why did you conspire against me with the son of Jesse by giving him food and a sword and by consulting God for him that he might rebel against me and become my enemy, as is the case today?' Ahimelech answered the king, 'Who among all your servants is as loyal as David, the king's son-in-law, captain of your bodyguard and honored in your own house?"* (11) Chapter 24 of 1 Samuel shows how David proved his loyalty.

In his Epistle to the Romans, Paul tells us, *"Let every person be subject to the governing authorities because there is no authority except from God, and those authorities that exist have been instituted by God. Therefore, whoever resists authority resists what God has appointed, and those who resist will incur judgment."* (12)

Christians should be the last to be heard leveling personal attacks on or name-calling the President, or the Governor, or the Mayor, or any other governmental leader placed over them. You may say that you live in a democracy and therefore have a right and responsibility to criticize your leaders. However, as members of the kingdom of God you have no such right. You have, rather, a command to obey and to pray for civil as well as religious authorities.

Beyond that you have the right, privilege, and responsibility to vote for better leaders, when the opportunity arises. If you don't vote, you have no right to complain.

(1) Judges 2:1-3
(2) Judges 2:10-19
(3) Proverbs 20:6
(4) A prophecy given at a Charismatic Conference in Kansas City, 1977
(5) Sirach 10:27 &28
(6) Deuteronomy 24:5
(7) 1 Timothy 3: 4 & 5
(8) Numbers 12:1-15
(9) Kansas City, 1977
(10) Daniel 6:1-5
(11) 1 Samuel 22:11-14
(12) Romans 13:1 & 2

UNDERSTANDING YOUR ENEMIES

The Devil or Satan

Once Jesus told this parable: *"The kingdom of Heaven may be compared to someone who sowed good seed in his field. While everyone was asleep, an enemy came and sowed weeds among the wheat and then went away. So, when the plants came up and bore grain, the weeds appeared as well. The slaves of the householder came and said to him, 'Master, did you not sow good seed in your field? Where, then, did these weeds come from?' He answered, 'An enemy has done this.'*

Then, Jesus *"left the crowds and went into the house. His disciples approached him, saying 'explain to us the parable of the weeds of the field.'*

"Jesus answered, 'The one who sows the good seed is the Son of Man, the field is the world, and the good seed is the children of the kingdom of Heaven. The weeds are the children of the evil one, and the enemy who sowed them is the devil." (1)

The devil or Satan is the first enemy you encounter when you come into the kingdom of Heaven. He is the *"prince of this world"* (2) who has *"the power of death"*. (3) *"He was a murderer from the beginning and does not stand in the truth because there is no truth in him. When he lies, he speaks according to his own nature because he is a liar and the father of lies."* (4)

Satan is the *"ruler of the power of the air, the spirit that is now at work among those who are disobedient."* (5) He *"disguises himself as an angel of light."* (6) He *"comes and takes away the word out of peoples' hearts so that they may not believe and be saved."* (7) Satan is the *"deceiver of the whole world."* (8) He is the accuser of Christians *"who accuses them night and day before our God."* (9)

50

When Jesus began his ministry, his first battle was with the devil: *"Jesus, full of the holy Spirit, returned from the Jordan and was led by the Spirit into the wilderness where, for forty days, he was tempted by the devil. He ate nothing at all during these days. When they were over, he was famished. The devil said to him, 'If you are the Son of God, command this stone to become a loaf of bread.'*

"Then, the devil led him up and showed him in an instant all the kingdoms of the world. The devil said to him, 'To you will I give their glory and all this authority for it has been given over to me, and I give it to anyone I please. If you, then, will worship me, it will all be yours.'

"Then, the devil took him to Jerusalem and placed him on the pinnacle of the temple, saying to him, 'If you are the Son of God, throw yourself down from here.' When the devil had finished every test, he departed from him until an opportune time." (10)

Because human beings lost dominion over all creation through original sin, Satan has now become the prince of this world. *"The god of this world has blinded the minds of the unbelievers to keep them from seeing the light of the gospel of the glory of Christ, who is the image of God."* (11)

So then, *"put on the full armor of God so as to be able to resist the devil's tactics because it is not against human enemies that you have to struggle but against the principalities and the ruling forces who are masters of the darkness in this world, the spirits of evil in the heavens. That is why you must take up all God's armor. You will not be able to put up any resistance on the evil day or stand your ground, even though you exert yourself to the full."* (12)

The World

What is meant by "the world?" The world includes all of creation that has not yet been redeemed from the effects of the sin of our first parents and brought under the Lordship of Jesus Christ. It is still in a fallen state and has its own identity. *"It was through one man (Adam) that sin came into the world, and through sin death. Thus, death has spread through the whole human race because everyone has sinned. Sin already existed in the world before there was any law."* (13)

The world includes all the destructive forces of nature as well as sicknesses and diseases of every kind. It also includes *"empty, seductive philosophies according to human tradition according to the elemental powers of the world."* Examples would be astrology, scientology, materialism, secularism, and relativism. (14) That is why, *"in dealing with their own kind, the children of this world are more astute than the children of light."* (15) But, *'the wisdom of this world is foolishness with God."* (16) *"God has made the wisdom of this world look foolish! As God in his wisdom ordained, the world failed to find him by its wisdom."* (17)

"To shame the wise, God has chosen what the world counts folly. To shame what is strong, God has chosen what the world counts weakness. He has chosen things without rank or standing in the world, mere nothings, to overthrow the existing order. So, no place is left for any pride in the presence of God." (18)

Do you know that *"friendship with the world is enmity with God? Whoever wishes to be a friend of the world becomes an enemy of God."* (19) *"You were dead through the transgressions and sins in which you once lived, following the course of this world, following the ruler of the power of the air, the spirit that is now at work among those who are disobedient. All of us once lived among them in the passions of our flesh, following the desires of flesh and senses, and we were by nature children of wrath like everyone else."* (20) *"When we were not of age, we were enslaved to the elemental powers of the world."* (21)

In the parable of the seeds, the thorns *"are the ones who hear the word, but the cares of the world, and the lure of wealth, and the desire for other things come in and choke the word and it yields nothing."* (22) *"If, after they have escaped the defilements of the world through the knowledge of our Lord and Savior Jesus Christ, they are again entangled in them and overpowered, the last state has become worse for them than the first. It would have been better for them never to have known the way of righteousness than, after knowing it, to turn back from the holy commandment that was passed on to them."* (23)

Therefore *"what profit is there for one to gain the whole world and forfeit his or her life? What could one give in exchange for his or her life?"* (24) *"Remember that you were at one time without Christ, having no hope and without God in the world."* (25) *"You were dead through the trespasses and sins in which you once lived, following the course of this world, following the ruler of the power of the air, the spirit that is now at work among those who are disobedient."* (26)

"Do not be conformed to this world but be transformed by the renewing of your mind so that you may discern the will of God - what is good and acceptable and perfect." (27) *"When we are judged by the Lord, we are disciplined so that we may not be condemned along with the world."* (28) *"Godly grief produces a repentance that leads to salvation and brings no regret, but worldly grief produces death."* (29) *"The saying is sure and worthy of full acceptance, that Christ Jesus came into the world to save sinners."* (30)

"We have received not the spirit of the world but the Spirit that is from God so that we may understand the gifts bestowed on us by God." (31) *"Do not love the world or the things of the world. The love of the Father is not in those who love the world because all that is in the world - the desire*

of the flesh, the desire of the eyes, the pride in riches - come not from the Father but from the world. The world and its desires are passing away, but those who do the will of God live forever." (32)

"In this way he has given us his promises, great beyond all price, so that through them we may escape the corruption with which lust has infected the world and may come to share in the very being of God." (33) *"See what love the Father has given us, that we should be called children of God. That is what we are. The reason the world does not know us is that it did not know him."* (34) *"This is the judgment, that the light has come into the world, and people loved darkness rather than light because their deeds are evil."* (35)

"All things are yours, whether the world or life or death or the present or the future - all belong to you, and you belong to Christ, and Christ belongs to God." (36) *"You are in the world but you do not belong to the world."* (37) *"Those who are rich in the world's goods should not be proud nor fix their hopes on so uncertain things as money but on God, who richly provides all things for us to enjoy."* (38)

"Religion that is pure and undefiled before God, the Father, is this: to care for orphans and widows in their distress and to keep oneself unstained by the world." (39) *"You are the light of the world. Let your light shine before others so that they may see your good works and give glory to your Father in Heaven."* (40)

Your Self

Your greatest enemy, and one of the hardest to overcome, is your self. *"It is what comes out of a person that defiles. It is from within, from the human heart, that evil intentions come: fornication, theft, murder, adultery, greed, wickedness, deceit, licentiousness, envy, slander, pride, and folly. All these evil things come from within, and they defile a person.* (41) *"The desires of self-indulgence are always in opposition to the Spirit, and the desires of the Spirit are in opposition to self-indulgence: they are opposites, one against the other. That is how you are prevented from doing the things you want to.*

"When self-indulgence is at work, the results are obvious: sexual vice, impurity, and sensuality, the worship of false gods and sorcery, antagonisms and rivalry, jealousy, bad temper and quarrels, disagreements, factions and malice, drunkenness, orgies, and all such things." (42)

"I do not understand my own actions. I do not do what I want but the very thing I hate. I know that nothing good dwells within me, that is, in my flesh. I can will what is right but cannot do it. I do not do the good I want, but the evil I do not want is what I do.

"So, I find it to be a law that, when I want to do what is good, evil

lies close at hand. I delight in the law of God in my innermost self, but I see in my members another law at war with the law of my mind, making me captive to the law of sin that dwells in my members. With my mind, I am a slave to the law of God, but within my flesh, I am a slave to the law of sin." (43)

"Put to death, then, the parts of you that are earthly: immorality, impurity, passion, evil desire, and the greed that is idolatry." (44) *"Get rid of such things: anger, wrath, malice, slander, and obscene language from your mouth. Do not lie."* (45) *"Put away your former way of life, your old self, corrupt and deluded by its lusts. Be renewed in the spirit of your mind and clothe yourself with the new self, created according to the likeness of God in true righteousness."* (46)

Godless People

"The children of God and the children of the devil are revealed in this way: all who do not do what is right are not from God, nor are those who do not love their brothers and sisters. Let no one deceive you. Everyone who does what is right is righteous, just as God is righteous. Everyone who commits sin is a child of the devil because the devil has been sinning from the beginning. The Son of God was revealed for this purpose, to destroy the works of the devil." (47)

"Many deceivers have gone out into the world, those who do not confess that Jesus Christ has come in the flesh. Any such person is the deceiver and the antichrist! (48) *"Who is the liar but the one who denies that Jesus is the Christ? This is the antichrist, the one who denies the Father and the Son."* (49)

"Certain intruders have stolen in among you, people who pervert the grace of God into licentiousness and deny our only Master and Lord, Jesus Christ." (50) *"In the same way, these deluded dreamers continue to defile their own bodies, flout authority, and insult celestial beings."* (51) *"These people slander whatever they do not understand."* (52) *"They are shepherds who take care only of themselves. They are clouds carried along by the wind without giving rain, trees fruitless in autumn, dead twice over, and pulled up by their roots."* (53)

"They are mischief makers, grumblers governed only by their own desires, with mouths full of boastful talk, ready to flatter others for gain." (54) They like to be leaders but will not pay any attention to other authority. They lie and deceive. They refuse hospitality to other brothers and sisters but keep those under them from receiving them, and indeed try to drive them out. (55)

False Prophets

"Anyone who is so 'progressive' as not to remain in the teaching of Christ does not have God. Whoever remains in the teaching has the Father and the Son. If anyone comes to you and does not bring this doctrine, do not receive him in your house or even greet him." (56)

Jesus said, *"Beware that no one leads you astray. Many will come in my Name, saying, 'I am the Messiah' and they will lead many astray."* (57) *"Many will say, 'I am he!' and 'the time is near!' Do not go after them."* (58)

"Many false prophets will arise and lead many astray. Because of the increase of lawlessness, the love of many will grow cold." (59) *"In the past there were also false prophets among the people, just as you will also have false teachers among you. They will introduce their destructive views, disowning the very Master who redeemed them and bringing swift destruction on their own heads. They will gain many adherents to their dissolute practices through whom the way of truth will be brought into disrepute. In their greed for money, they will trade on your credulity with their fabrications.*

"With their high-sounding but empty talk, they tempt back people who have scarcely escaped from those who live in error by playing on the disordered desires of their human nature and by debaucheries. They may promise freedom but are themselves slaves to corruption because, if anyone lets himself be dominated by anything, then he or she is a slave to it." (60)

"Such boasters are false apostles, deceitful workers, disguising themselves as apostles of Christ. And, no wonder! Even Satan disguises himself as an angel of light! So, it is not strange if his ministers also disguise themselves as ministers of righteousness." (61)

"Beware of false prophets who come to you in sheep's clothing but inwardly are ravenous wolves. You will know them by their fruits." (62) Yes they will look like Christians on the outside. They will proclaim their Christianity loudly and will appear to be very spiritual and "charismatic." But, discern carefully the fit from the counterfeit. On the inside, they are really like wolves that are bent on devouring the sheep. The principle here is that you will know them by what they do. Behavior is an expression of one's attitude. Observe their behavior carefully and see what kind of fruit it is producing.

"Beloved, do not trust every spirit but test the spirits to see whether they belong to God because many false prophets have gone out into the world. This is how you can know the Spirit of God: every spirit that acknowledges Jesus Christ come in the flesh belongs to God, and every spirit that does not acknowledge Jesus does not belong to God. This is the spirit of the antichrist that, as you heard, is to come but, in fact, is already in the world. They belong to the world; accordingly, their teaching belongs

to the world, and the world belongs to them." (63)

"Whoever teaches otherwise and does not agree with the sound words of our Lord Jesus Christ and the teaching that is in accordance with godliness is conceited, understands nothing, and has a morbid craving for controversy and for disputes about words. From these come envy, dissension, slander, base suspicion, and wrangling among those who are depraved in mind and bereft of the truth, imagining that godliness is a means of gain." (64)

Brothers And Sisters

"Jesus began to show his disciples that he must go to Jerusalem and undergo great suffering at the hands of the elders and chief priests and scribes, and be killed, and on the third day be raised. Peter took him aside and began to rebuke him, saying, 'God forbid it, Lord! This must never happen to you.' But, he turned and said to Peter, 'Get behind me, Satan! You are a stumbling block to me for you are setting your mind not on divine things but on human things." (65)

"Another time, Jesus answered them, 'Did I not choose you, the twelve. Yet, one of you is a devil.' He was speaking of Judas, son of Simon Iscariot because he, though one of the twelve, was going to betray him." (66)

Jesus and his disciples were at supper. *"The devil had already put into the heart of Judas, son of Simon Iscariot, to betray him."* (67) *"After he received the piece of bread, Satan entered into him."* (68) *"He went and conferred with the chief priests and officers of the temple police about how he might betray Jesus to them."* (69)

Jesus has warned us: *"I have come to set a man against his father, a daughter against her mother, a daughter-in-law against her mother-in-law. One's enemies will be members of one's own household."* (70)

"From now on, five in one household will be divided, three against two and two against three. A father will be divided against his son and a son against his father, a mother against her daughter and a daughter against her mother, a mother-in-law against her daughter-in-law and a daughter-in-law against her mother-in-law." (71)

"Brother will betray brother to death, and a father his child. Children will rise against parents and have them put to death. All will hate you because of my Name. But, the one who endures to the end will be saved." (72)

"Do not associate with anyone who bears the name of brother or sister (in Christ) who is sexually immoral or greedy, or is an idolater, reviler, drunkard, or robber. Do not even eat with such a one--not at all meaning the immoral of this world, or the greedy and robbers, or idolaters,

since you would need to go out of the world." (73)

"Do you not know that the unjust will not inherit the kingdom of God? Do not be deceived. Neither fornicators nor idolaters nor adulterers nor boy prostitutes nor practicing homosexuals nor robbers will inherit the Kingdom of God." (74)

Demonic Spirits

Demons, or evil spirits, are created spiritual beings who fell from Heaven with Satan and who are under his control. Like humans, they possess intellect and will. They take up residence in living creatures, including humans, where they are allowed to dwell or into which they are sent. They have no power or authority of their own; they must take orders from elsewhere. They will obey whoever commands them, that is, Satan, their boss; Jesus, Satan's boss; or Christians, in the Name of Jesus.

"When an evil spirit or demon has gone out of a person, it wanders through waterless regions looking for a resting place, but it finds none. Then, it says, 'I will return to my house from which I came.' When it comes, it finds it empty, swept, and put in order. Then, it goes and brings along seven other spirits more evil than itself, and they enter and live there. The last state of that person is worse than the first." (75)

Demons or evil spirits are generally regarded as hostile to God and to human beings and, therefore, evil. They may be the cause of bad influences such as disease and mental distress on human beings. They can attach to a personality either through traumatic events, even in pre-birth or early life, or willfully through involvement with occult practices such as Ouija boards, witchcraft, card laying, and horoscopes. Whatever part of you is not under the willing control of Jesus and his Holy Spirit is open to the control of Satan and his spirits. Thus, you can be afflicted with or oppressed by an evil spirit, even if you are a Christian, because of previous influences.

However, if you submit your will to Jesus, you have the same authority he has over evil spirits, all sickness and diseases, and all other destructive forces of this world. You can be delivered of them by a mature Christian, or cast them out of yourself, after you confess (agree with God that it is wrong), renounce (firmly reject) them, and repent of (actively turn away from) any opening you gave to them. You must also forgive whoever may have opened you up to their influence, including especially yourself. Then, in the Name of Jesus and by his precious blood, command them to leave you.

"I have given you the power to 'tread upon serpents' and scorpions and upon the full force of the enemy, and nothing will harm you." (76)

"These signs will accompany those who believe: by using my Name they will cast out demons. They will speak in new tongues. They will pick up

snakes, and if they drink any deadly thing, it will not hurt them. They will lay their hands on the sick, and they will recover." (77)

Summary

"We know that we are God's children and that the whole world lies under the power of the evil one." (78) *"God put his power to work in Christ when he raised him from the dead and seated him at his right hand in the heavenly places, far above all rule and authority and power and dominion and above every name that is named, not only in this age but also in the age to come. He has put all things under his feet and has made him the Head over all things for the Church, which is his Body, the fullness of him who fills all in all."* (79)

"When you were dead in trespasses and the un-circumcision of your flesh, God made you alive together with him, when he forgave you all your trespasses, erasing the record that stood against you with its legal demands. He set this aside, nailing it to the Cross. He disarmed the rulers and authorities and made a public example of them, triumphing over them in it." (80)

"See to it that no one takes you captive through philosophy and empty deceit, according to human tradition, according to the elemental spirits of the universe and not according to Christ." (81)

Rather, *"build yourself upon your most holy faith, pray in the Holy Spirit, keep yourself in the love of God, and look forward to the mercy of our Lord Jesus Christ that leads to eternal life. Have mercy on some who are wavering, save others by snatching them out of the fire, and have mercy on still others with fear."* (82)

"To the one who is able to keep you from stumbling and to present you unblemished and exultant in the presence of his glory, to the only God, our Savior, through Jesus Christ our Lord be glory, majesty, power, and authority from ages past, now, and for ages to come. Amen." (83)

(1) Matthew 13:24-28a, 36-39a
(2) John 14:30
(3) Hebrews 2:14c
(4) John 8:44
(5) Ephesians 2:2
(6) 2 Corinthians 11:14
(7) Luke 8:11
(8) Revelation 12:9a
(9) Revelation 12:10b
(10) Luke 4:1-3, 5-7, 9, 13
(18) 1 Corinthians 1:27-29
(19) James 4:4
(20) Ephesians 2:1-3
(21) Galatians 4:3
(22) Mark 4:18-19
(23) 2 Peter 2:20-21
(24) Matthew 8:36-37
(25) Ephesians 2:12
(26) Ephesians 2:2
(27) Romans 12:2
(28) 1 Corinthians 11:32

(11) 2 Corinthians 4:4
(12) Ephesians 6:11-13
(13) Romans 5:12-13
(14) Colossians 2:8
(15) Luke 15:8b
(16) 1 Corinthians 3:19
(17) 1 Corinthians
1:20b-21a

(37) John 17:11, 14
(38) 1 Timothy 6:17
(39) James 1:27
(40) Matthew 5:14, 16
(41) Mark 7:20-23
(42) Galatians 5:17-19
(43) Romans 7:15, 18-19,
21-21
(44) Colossians- 3:5
(45) Colossians 3:8-91
(46) Ephesians 4:22-24
(47) 1 John 3:10, 7-8

(48) 2 John 7
(49) 1 John 2:22
(50) Jude 4
(51) Jude 8
(52) Jude 10a
(53) Jude 12
(54) Jude 16
(55) 3 John 9-10
(56) 2 John 9-10
(57) Matthew 24:4-5
(58) Luke 21:8
(59) Matthew 24:11-12
(60) 2 Peter 2:1-3a,
2:18-19
(61) 2 Corinthians
11:13-15

(29) 2 Corinthians 7:10
(30) 1 Timothy 1:15
(31) 1 Corinthians 2:12
(32) 1 John 2:15-17
(33) 1 Peter 1:3
(34) 1 John 3:1
(35) 1 John 3:19
(36) 1 Corinthians 3:22b-23

(62) Matthew 7:15-17
(63) 1 John 4:1-3, 5
(64) 1 Timothy 6:3-5
(65) Matthew 15:21-23
(66) John 6:70-71
(67) John 13:2
(68) John 13:27a
(69) Luke 22:4
(70) Matthew 10:35-36
(71) Luke 12:52-53
(72) Matthew 10:21-22
(73) 1 Corinthians 5:11-12
(74) 1 Corinthians 6:9-10
(75) Matthew 12:43-45
(76) Luke 10:19
(77) Mark 16:17-18
(78) 1 John 5:19
(79) Ephesians 1:20-23
(80) Colossians 2:13-15
(81) Colossians 2:8
(82) Jude 20-22
(83) Jude 24-25

A LOOK AT YOUR WEAPONS

"We live as human beings but do not wage war according to human standards because the weapons of our warfare are not merely human; they have the power to destroy strongholds. We destroy arguments and every proud obstacle that is raised up against the knowledge of God and take every thought captive to obey Christ. (1)

"Draw your strength from the Lord and from his mighty power. Put on the armor of God so that you may be able to stand firm against the tactics of the devil. Our struggle is not with flesh and blood but with the principalities, with the powers, with the world rulers of this present darkness, with the evil spirits in the heavens. Therefore, put on the armor of God so that you may be able to resist on the evil day and, having done everything, to hold your ground. Stand fast with your loins girded in truth, clothed with righteousness as a breastplate, and your feet shod in readiness for the gospel of peace. In all circumstances, hold faith as a shield to quench all flaming arrows of the evil one. Take the helmet of salvation and the sword of the Spirit, which is the Word of God. With all prayer and supplication, pray at every opportunity in the Spirit. To that end be watchful with all perseverance and supplication for all the holy ones." (2)

Let's take a closer look at some of the weapons mentioned here as well as some others of which Scripture speaks.

The Word Of God

After Jesus was led into the wilderness and fasted for forty days and forty nights, he was famished. Thus, he was vulnerable in his flesh. Satan took advantage of this and tempted him three times. What Satan didn't know was that, because he had been spending time with his Father during this time, Jesus was powerful in his spirit. So, three times Jesus said to Satan "IT IS WRITTEN" and quoted the Word of God to him. (3)

The Word of God is the most powerful weapon we have been given in our arsenal. It never goes forth empty but accomplishes all that it is sent to do. The Word of God and the Spirit of God always go together. The Word without the Spirit is a dead letter; the Spirit without the word is simply wind. But, when the Word and the Spirit combine, there is life-giving power in any situation, and nothing can resist it. That is why the Word of God is called the sword of the Spirit. That is also why it is critical to study and understand the Word of God correctly, that is, the Spirit must confirm it. As he always does, Satan misquoted and distorted the meaning of God's Word to Jesus, and nothing happened. Jesus quoted the Word correctly, and *"the devil left him"*. (4) Thus, James says, *"submit yourselves to God, resist the devil, and he will flee from you."* (5)

Persevering Prayer

"Pray without ceasing." (6) Jesus told a parable about the need to pray always and not to lose heart. He said, *"In a certain city there was a judge who neither feared God nor had respect for people. In that city, there was a widow who kept coming to him and saying, 'Grant me justice against my opponent.' For a while. he refused but later said to himself, 'Though I have no fear of God nor respect for anyone, yet because this widow keeps bothering me, I will grant her justice so that she may not wear me out by continually coming.' The Lord said, 'Listen to what the unjust judge says. Will not God grant justice to his chosen ones who cry to him day and night? Will he delay long in helping them?'"* (7)

Jesus said, *"Ask, and it will be given you; search, and you will find; knock, and the door will be opened for you. Everyone who asks receives, everyone who searches finds, and for everyone who knocks, the door will be opened."* (8)

Forgiveness

Forgiveness does not always change the other person but does change you. Forgiveness releases you from any bondage or holds of anger and hurt that you may feel because of what you perceive that someone says or does to you. Thus it gives you freedom. If the person who has offended you receives and accepts your forgiveness, then there is reconciliation and the potential for reestablishing a relationship. Jesus forgave us on the Cross. When we received and accepted his forgiveness, we were reconciled to him, and a new life and relationship began. This is what salvation means.

"When you stand to pray, forgive anyone against whom you have a

grievance so that your heavenly Father may in turn forgive you your transgressions. (9) *If your brother or sister sins, rebuke him or her. If he or she repents, forgive him or her.* (10) *If the same person sins against you seven times a day, and turns back to you seven times and says, 'I repent', you must forgive.* (11) *If you forgive others their transgressions, your heavenly Father will forgive you. If you do not forgive others, neither will your Father forgive your transgressions."* (12)

Unwavering Faith

"Faith is the assurance of things hoped for, the conviction of things not seen. Without faith it is impossible to please God." (13) Jesus said, *"If you do not doubt in your heart but believe that what you say will come to pass, it will be done for you. I tell you, whatever you ask for in prayer, believe that you have received it, and it will be yours."* (14)

Unwavering faith means to take God at his word and to not ask questions.

Blessing

To bless means to use your authority to speak words of life and faith over someone with the intent of positively impacting the person's life. *"People were bringing little children to Jesus in order that he might touch them. He took them up in his arms, laid his hands on them, and blessed them."* (15)

As he was getting ready to return to the Father after his resurrection, Jesus led his disciples as far as Bethany. *"Lifting up his hands, he blessed them. While he was blessing them, he withdrew from them and was carried up into Heaven."* (16)

"From the same mouth come blessing and cursing. My brothers and sisters, this ought not to be so. (17) *Bless those who curse you, pray for those who abuse you.* (18) *Bless those who persecute you; bless and do not curse them."* (19)

Summary

You have a mighty spiritual arsenal at your disposal.

But, you must train yourself in their use as any true soldier does. They are powerful and effective against any type of enemy you may face,physical,financial, mental, or spiritual. With them, you and Jesus are an overwhelming majority!

(1) 2 Corinthians 10:3-5   (11) Luke 17:4

(2) Ephesians 6:10-18
(3) Matthew 4:4, 7, 10
(4) Matthew 4:11a
(5) James 4:7
(6) 1 Thessalonians 5:17
(7) Luke 18:1-7
(8) Luke 11:9-10
(9) Mark 11:25 & 26
(10) Luke 17:3

(12) Matthew 6:14-15
(13) Hebrews 11:1, 6a
(14) Mark 11:23b-24
(15) Mark 10:13a, 16
(16) Luke 24:50-51
(17) James 3:10
(18) Luke 6:28
(19) Romans 12:14

MARCHING ORDERS

A Christian disciple is one who is totally committed to following and serving the Lord Jesus Christ. Luke 10 outlines seven basic instructions that it is important for disciples to carry out.

Note, however, the two conditions for being called to this task. Verse 1 says the Lord *appointed* and he *sent out*. Know that the Lord Jesus Christ appoints you and that he is sending you out. When God calls someone, he always equips that person before he sends the person out. Never go in your own power. This book is designed to help equip you. Jesus says in another place, "*You did not choose me but I chose you and appointed you to go and bear fruit, fruit that will last.* (1) Notice also where he is sending you: "*to every town and place where he himself intended to visit.*" (2) Then, study the instructions that Jesus gives to his disciples before he sends them out.

ASK THE LORD FOR LABORERS - As a disciple, you must be a man or woman of prayer. Personal prayer is the lifeline to God and the means by which he primarily speaks to and directs you. But, you must also be an intercessor. You must pray for others. Intercessory prayer is God's means for accomplishing his purposes in the world. Jesus indicates one purpose for which he wants you to intercede: "*The harvest is plentiful, but the laborers are few. Therefore, ask the Lord of the harvest to send out laborers into his harvest.* (3)

GO - Verse 3 says, "*Go on your way. See, I am sending you out like lambs into the midst of wolves.*" You must go when the Lord says go and stop when he says stop; and you must know the difference. When he says go, you must obey immediately. The previous chapter describes in vivid terms would-be disciples who choose to follow the Lord on their own terms and timetables: "*As they were proceeding on their journey, someone said to him, 'I will follow you wherever you go.' Jesus answered him, 'Foxes have dens and birds of the sky have nests, but the Son of Man has nowhere to rest his head.' To another, he said, 'Follow me.' But, he replied, 'Let me go first and bury my father.' Jesus answered him, 'Let the dead bury their dead. You go and proclaim the kingdom of God.' Another said, 'I will follow you, Lord, but first let me say farewell to my family at home.' Jesus said, 'No one who sets a hand to the plow and looks to what was left behind is fit for the kingdom of God.'* (4)

"Then, he said to them all, 'If any want to become my followers, let them deny themselves and take up their cross daily and follow me. Those who want to save their life will lose it. Those who lose their life for my sake will save it. What does it profit them if they gain the whole world but lose or forfeit themselves? Those who are ashamed of me and of my words, of them the Son of Man will be ashamed when he comes in his glory and the glory of the Father and of the holy angels.'" (5)

Now, in order to go quickly when the Lord says "go," you must travel light, be single-minded, and depend completely on God. Would-be disciples are preoccupied with their own priorities. Jesus says, *"Carry no purse, no bag, no sandals, and greet no one on the road."* (6)

According to Deuteronomy 25:9ff, sandals were proverbially a man's cheapest possession. Therefore, "a man without sandals" was the poorest of the poor. In Exodus, the Israelites were to eat with their loins girt, sandals on their feet, and their staff in hand, like those who were in flight. The principle, in any case, is that Jesus requires a total dependency on God for food and shelter. Only when you get to where the Lord is sending you are you to stop and socialize.

STAY PUT - Accept what is given to you or provided for you. *"Whatever house you enter, first say, 'Peace to this house!' If anyone is there who shares in peace, your peace will rest on that person. If not, it will return to you. Remain in the same house, eating and drinking whatever they provide because the laborer deserves to be paid. Do not move about from house to house."* (7)

MINISTER THE WORD AND THE SPIRIT - In Luke 9:11, Jesus received the crowds that followed him, spoke to them about the kingdom of God, and healed those who needed to be cured. In Luke 9:42 Jesus rebuked an unclean spirit, healed a boy, and returned him to his father. In this chapter, Jesus commands his disciples to do the same: *"Whenever you enter a town, and its people welcome you, eat what is set before you; cure the sick who are there and say to them, 'The kingdom of God is at hand for you."* (8)

KNOW WHEN TO MOVE ON - Not everyone will accept your ministry, anymore than everyone accepted the ministry of Jesus. If you have been obedient to the above instructions, you are not responsible for the outcome. The one who receives your ministry or rejects it, is. Thus, Jesus says, "*Whenever you enter a town, and they do not welcome you, go out into its streets and say, 'Even the dust of your town that clings to our feet we wipe off in protest against you. Yet, know this: the kingdom of God is at hand for you.'*" (9)

KNOW YOUR AUTHORITY AND STAND ON IT - Jesus says to his disciples, "*Whoever listens to you listens to me. Whoever rejects you rejects me. Whoever rejects me rejects the one who sent me.*" (10) When Jesus sends you out, he is present in you. You are his hands and his mouth. Your authority is his authority, and his authority extends over all creation: below the earth, on the earth, and above the earth as we have already seen. Jesus says, "*I watched Satan fall from Heaven like a flash of lightning. See, I have given you authority to tread on snakes and scorpions and over all the power of the enemy; and nothing will hurt you.*" (11)

He is speaking here of demons and evil spirits as well as of Satan himself. The authority of the true disciple is as extensive as the authority of the Lord Jesus himself. What we could accomplish if we could only grasp this truth! Satan's kingdom would fall before us in a minute if we could only believe this! God is preparing us for this, however, and it will happen.

REJOICE - "*Do not rejoice at this, that the spirits submit to you, but rejoice that your names are written in Heaven.*" (12) "*Rejoice in the Lord always; again I will say, Rejoice,*" Paul exclaims to the Philippians. (13) As if to set the example,

"*At that very hour Jesus rejoiced in the Holy Spirit.*" (14) In his joy, Jesus says to you as he said to those first disciples, "*Blessed are the eyes that see what you see! I tell you that many prophets and kings desired to see what you see but did not see it, and to hear what you hear but did not hear it.*" (15)

(1) John 15:16	(9) Luke 10:10-11
(2) Luke 10:1	(10) Luke 10:16
(3) Luke 10:2	(11) Luke 10:18-19
(4) Luke 9:57-62	(12) Luke 10:20
(5) Luke 9:23-26	(13) Philippians 4:4
(6) Luke 10:4	(14) Luke 10:21
(7) Luke 10:5-7	(15) Luke 10:23-24
(8) Luke 10:8-9	

CPSIA information can be obtained at www.ICGtesting.com
Printed in the USA
BVOW08s1957020915

416312BV00001B/38/P